THE WEDDING DRESS

THE WEDDING DRESS
Meditations on Word and Life

FANNY HOWE

UNIVERSITY OF CALIFORNIA PRESS
BERKELEY · LOS ANGELES · LONDON

University of California Press
Berkeley and Los Angeles, California

University of California Press, Ltd.
London, England

© 2003 by The Regents of the University of California

Library of Congress Cataloging-in-Publication Data

Howe, Fanny.
   The wedding dress : meditations on word and life /
Fanny Howe.
        p.   cm.
   Includes bibliographical references.
   ISBN 0-520-23625-4 (alk. paper). — ISBN 0-520-23840-0
(pbk. : alk paper)
   I. Title.

PS3558.O89W43   2003
811'.54—dc 20   2003050706
                                       CIP

12   11   10   09   08   07   06   05   04   03
10   9   8   7   6   5   4   3   2   1

It was the truth but still not quite.

Ilona Karmel

CONTENTS

INTRODUCTION

My children and I grew up together in Jamaica Plain—a section of Boston that lies between Jamaica Pond and Franklin Park. The children went to the local public schools, then in the process of desegregation, and I went to school as a low-level instructor of creative writing. My adult life began when I met their father in late 1967, only a few months after my father had died of a heart attack. I had been working for CORE (the Congress on Racial Equality) in Roxbury. At first I traveled south with a friend to report on goings-on down there; we went through Mississippi and Selma, Natchez and the Carolinas. Later I returned to Boston to continue working for CORE. My partner in seeking out housing violations and reporting them was Jonathan Kozol, who later introduced me to Carl Senna with the warning, "Don't fall in love with him."

Carl was a writer and I was also writing and editing with Bill Corbett the small magazine called *Fire Exit*. We accepted a good story written by Carl, who lived on Massachusetts Avenue near Columbus Avenue in a building occupied mostly by prostitutes. His apartment was shrouded in blackness with hardly enough light available to see the few political posters on the wall. His front door wore his name on a card: *Carlos Francisco Jose Senna*. His father had been a boxer, a Mexican, deported from the U.S.A. and returned to Sierra Leone under Nixon's Wetback Laws. His mother, African-American, had moved to Boston from the South where she had been a schoolteacher and piano player.

Carl had almost finished at Boston University but was now working as an attendant in a mental hospital, where he was shocked by the abuse of the patients. His mother lived in the Whittier Street projects with his sister and brother, both of them grown and en route to independent lives. It didn't take me long to become involved with Carl and his family, but it was a couple of months before our relationship changed into a romance. We were married a year after Kozol's warning, and had our first child exactly nine months later. We would have three children within four years, and I would spend the seven years of our tumultuous marriage in a skewed relationship to many old friends and family members. Not one of them was rude or overtly racist. But the media and the environs around Boston were so charged with those exact possibilities that any personal exchange on the subject of home life would be marked with symbolic value.

Both of us were needy and uprooted when we met. I was even worse than that: crippled by claustrophobia, riddled with terror attacks, overcome by shyness, and strangely afraid of human beings—especially those in any position of authority. Carl had no direction as far as a career went, and so we grabbed onto each other in an effort at stabilizing ourselves. It had always been my immersion in the political chaos of those days (and in earlier days, side by side, with my father) that had awakened me to the possibility that I was feeling justifiable despair, not depression; social outrage, not personal anxiety. I was liberated from my own personality to talk and think and walk politics. Carl's and my shared interest in political philosophies (Paolo Freire, Ivan Illich, Franz Fanon) drew us together as much as anything else, and his experience with race and class issues became my education. My father had been a civil-rights activist and my personal ally as well. I missed him. It was always like "one of the comforts of home" to immerse myself in politics.

There were many women like me—born into white privilege but with no financial security, given a good education but no training for survival. Some of us ended up in cults, some in jail, some in far-out marriages. The daughters of white activists tended to become more engaged than even their fathers were, and like certain Greek heroines they drove themselves to madness and incarceration, carrying to the nth degree their fathers' progressive positions. Because my family (academic, artistic) had no extra money, there was no cushion for the crash from a comfortable home into the literal cold streets. Somehow Carl and I did manage to carve a niche for ourselves—through marriage and new jobs luckily acquired—just off the streets. We were both somewhat conservative in our habits. No narcotics, no rock 'n roll. Crossing the racial divide was the only radical ingredient in what we were doing. Basically we were in hiding when we weren't working.

+ + +

Carl was Catholic and his mother, who lived with us, was devout, attending daily Mass on her way to work at the courthouse downtown. We had the children baptized and I began attending Mass with my mother-in-law hovering at the back of the church, and feeling myself excluded and estranged from the rituals. I read Simone Weil, the Boff brothers, Gustavo Gutierrez and a variety of contemporary liberation theologians who incorporated socialist ideals with a Christian preferential option for the poor. And as the children grew older, each took catechism classes and first communion. I grew increasingly comfortable sitting at Mass and participating in everything but the Eucharist, for many years. The skepticism that was like a splash of iodine in the milk of my childhood home began to work its way out of my system.

Encircling this rather quiet and interior domestic quest was the city of Boston and its racist and violent rejection of progress, desegregation, dialogue. Louise Day Hicks and the vociferous Boston Irish were like the dogs and hoses in the South. No difference. Boston, always segregated into pockets of furious chauvinism—from the North End to the South—from rich white sections of Cambridge to poor working-class areas there—did not know how to separate issues of race and class. The poor were set against the poor, while the rich continued to glide around the periphery dispensing moral judgments.

Martin Luther King, Jr., was assassinated during the same season I met Carl. Parts of the city were cordoned off. James Brown was called in. We went to his concert, which had been organized to ward off riots and which succeeded. Although Boston never exploded to the same extent as other cities, the surge of Black Power was unlike anything that had happened there or in the country before. Blackness became the club that many whites longed to join. The raised fists, the street signals, the attitude, the rhetoric, the music—all these produced a change in white consciousness that had the effect of making whites defensive and aggressive on the one hand, or yearning for conciliation on the other.

It's an old story by now—how Black Power forced individual whites to see themselves as unstable and isolated social products, people who were at the end of the line and who were not the transcendent and eternal beings they had been raised to believe themselves to be. In those days it was a terrible blow to a mass ego. Whites, without even knowing it, had been getting away with murder. The fundamental assumption that they deserved everything they had, or didn't yet have, simply because they were white, had to be rethought. Any knowledge of the history of civil rights in this country would quickly expose race as a national obsession from day one—race as the way to measure intellectual superiority, that is. Mountains of documents supported this belief in white superiority; the very size of the heap revealed the desperate anxiety behind the claims. The Black Power movement showed how quickly and thoroughly a change of self-image can produce a radical reappraisal by one's neighbors, not to mention oneself; this lesson in identity politics ultimately blasted apart many fixed constructs.

Boston, recalcitrant and class-divided, was a poor choice of a place to live as a mixed couple. Even the most enlightened white academics had no black friends, or tokens only, and fled quickly to the suburbs for the schools. Those who stayed and struggled in the inner city were few and far between, and were both self-interested and heroic. They renovated houses in the South End and Jamaica Plain and involved themselves in school committees and busing and clinics and they did so with the social optimism of an earlier, pre-War generation. Yet many of them had no black friends at the end of the day, only colleagues in the battle for better schools for their children. In the black community there was very little agreement on anything, and because it was a small and old community, hatreds that take time to thrive had taken root, and the disagreements on social action were irreconcilable.

Boston's white upper class was divided between the Republican core group, who were in business, banking, and law, and who owned property in the suburbs, and Democrats, who didn't own much of anything and stayed in the realm of "letters" and political policy, social justice, and academics. Both groups came from Old Money, but the Democrats only had snuffboxes, tea cups, and dusty portraits to show for it, while the Republicans had long driveways, trees, and country clubs where blacks and Jews had been unwelcome for years. These two groups didn't speak and were socially divided into small mutually interested tiers. Even today, stockbrokers see other stockbrokers; academics see other academics. Doctors talk to doctors, and teachers are too tired at the end of the day to talk to anyone but their families. There is very little cross-cultural exchange even at the most privileged level in Boston. From that point down, the divisions have enlarged and darkened and continue to enlarge and darken.

+ + +

Boston is a parochial and paranoid city; it doesn't admit its own defects, and it belittles its own children as a result. It is a difficult city for African Americans. In Boston, as in much of America, there has always been more interracial interaction among the poor, the working class, churchgoing people, and criminals, including the Mafia, than among the rich and privileged. When self-interest includes racial crossings, in order to sustain certain vital social transactions, then there is more intermarriage too. In Boston, in the early and mid-seventies, there was a group of young, disenfranchised flower children who also intermarried; they were street poets and musicians. They took drugs; they crossed over. But most of them were already breaking apart and going in different directions around the time Nixon was impeached.

My children grew up with other racially mixed children who came out of that period. *Sesame Street* was their imaginary Cuba—an urban utopia that influenced their values for life. By 1980 almost all of their parents had divorced; their single white mothers ran their lives. Until those divorces it was as if we occupied a fleet of little arks that rose with the flood and tossed and sank; and inside our windowless habitats we blamed all the chaos on our marriages. Race war was enacted inside the tight little houseboats—violent language, violent action, intimidation, insult, accusations that made no sense, based as they were in an absolute lack of understanding of each others' cultures—all this in order to create a new society. We went so far out, we passed—on the way—insights and possibilities that were good as well as bad; there are worldly journeys that travel to the end of the possible; they are hellish passions; you learn everything from them.

After a few months of marriage and pregnancy, we moved to a small town on the Salem Harbor, north of Boston. We lived at the top of a very sheer short hill, called Sunset Road, that looked down onto the harbor. Carl's mother moved in with us, commuting by bus to her job to Boston, and we both had teaching jobs at Tufts University. Our decision to leave Boston was based in a certain self-consciousness about our marriage; our home was a hideout. But we had friends who visited us there: the African novelist Ayi Kwei Armah, his then-wife Fatima Mernissi, two friends Joe and Lynn Long (also a mixed marriage), whom we had met in New Mexico, Robert Creeley, and other new and old friends from Boston and New York. The talk steered invariably towards politics and race.

Carl got work in Boston again, now as an editor at Beacon Press, so—much to my mother-in-law's sorrow—we returned to the city. In Jamaica Plain we lived in a large white house on a street called Robeson Street that ran up Sumner Hill to Franklin Park, one of Olmsted's most glorious landscapes. Trees from this parkland spread huge branches over our house and the puddingstone juttings that supported the enormous and shabby Victorian houses on this one street. Roxbury's Hill district has a similar quality, and there are probably five streets in Jamaica Plain that remain in this condition. We loved the house and filled it with Carl's family and Jamaican, Irish, and African friends of friends who needed temporary housing. I helped establish the neighborhood health clinic and became close to the people on the streets around, and we started a day-care center in our basement, with two teachers and twelve little children, two of them mine; my third was still a baby beside me. In larger Boston, following on Arthur Garrity's court order to the city schools, the black community was developing Operation Exodus, METCO, the Bridge, and Catholic Bridge, programs designed to lift black children out of the inner city and place them in suburban, private, and parochial schools. Blacks and whites together were also organizing magnet schools in certain deprived districts of the city.

At night I would leave a pot of rice on the stove for people passing through. There were beans, vegetables, and the sound of Motown blasting. The children had a nursery in the attic where they developed intense fantasy lives around their dolls and stuffed animals and my mother-in-law had a bedroom between ours and theirs, where two cribs sat side-by-side and the baby girls conversed in coos and whispers. My mother-in-law, a small dark-skinned woman with sloe eyes and a large mischievous smile, continued to work all day at the courthouse and then returned to help me (like a husband!) in the evenings; but a cancer she had treated with a mastectomy began returning and she became increasingly crippled with pain in the following months. She died two months before I gave birth to my third child. Her illness— and finally her dying—profoundly affected our family. We were never the same without her, and the whole operation disintegrated in terrible ways. It was as if things from outdoors began to grow inside the house, under the tables and in the sinks.

This was a fertile but lonely time. While I was involved in neighborhood politics and my true colleagues were other mothers, racial tensions in the city subtly invaded the household. More frequently than not I found my point of view no longer fit that of my friends, even though we were committed to the same issues. Some worldview was inexorably shifting in me, and I felt sidelined by conversations and remarks that would have slid by unnoticed before. Many whites were demonstrating against Vietnam and much of the hot talk around that topic spilled into defenses and condemnations of underground organizations that believed in violent resistance. The four assassinations (the Kennedys, Malcom X, and Martin Luther King Jr.) had changed the entire atmosphere of political debate in the country from polite reasoning to justifications for revenge. The Cuban revolution and the liberation of African nations had already indicated to many of us that the only way to produce radical social change was to push the discourse to a criminal-inclusive language.

I quickly learned that white people are obsessed with race, and the subject comes up at least once in any three- or four-hour gathering. One night I went to a small town in Massachusetts to give a reading, and when I entered the room where an all-white group of people had gathered afterwards, they were saying, "If the lines ever get drawn, and the situation gets seriously violent, I know which side I will be on." And then they began to speak (liberals, all of them) about their fear of blacks, and their judgments of blacks, and I had to announce to them that my husband and children were black, before hastily departing.

This event has been repeated so many times, in multiple forms, that by now I make some kind of give-away statement after entering a white-only room, one way or the other, that will warn the people there "which side I am on." The situation most recently repeated itself about a hundred times in my presence over the subject of O.J. Simpson. His name was like the whistle of a train coming down the line, and I knew what was coming—vindictive racialized remarks, coming from otherwise socially progressive white people. You would think that he had organized mass murders and guerilla warfare on American streets. Louis Farrakhan is the only other public person who produces the same reaction. On these occasions, more than any others, I feel that my skin is white but my soul is not, and that I am in camouflage. It is clear to me that black men are in a no-win situation in relation to whites, including liberals who perceive them (but never say so) as sell-outs from their "own people" (not revolutionary enough) if they live with a white woman, and who then judge them as dangerous and anti-integrationist if they live with a black woman. It is the white envy of (and fetishization of) black men that has sustained the institution of racism. Integration is not a word that is heard anymore; incarceration has replaced it. Only white women in this country have historically been condemned to a lower status than black men, and that was when they crossed over and married black men. Then they were officially, legally, relegated to the lowest social caste. Many times people stopped me with my children, to ask, "Are they yours?" with an expression of disgust and disbelief on their faces. These were white people. In neighborhoods where there were Puerto Rican families with a wide range of colors and hair types among them, I felt safe; I was addressed in Spanish.

When they were very young, my children decided that they were black despite their fair skin and mestizo features. They decided this, with the help of their father, me, and the city of Boston at the height of the busing crisis, when the school system divided families according to each child's physical appearance. We decided that race was more a tribal than an individual choice, and we shared our views on this score with the children.

After my third child was in my arms I began to feel that I contained in my body a fourth child, and sometimes I would hallucinate, hearing the sound of this missing child crying. In some way this sensation began to correspond to the experience of "covering" and soon I could honestly and deeply feel myself to contain another self, a shadow.

There were at this time in Boston "women's groups" where small gatherings of friends would meet to talk about the condition of being female, of mothering and marrying. These groups more often revealed economic differences between us than ties that bound us, and they often wound up (disappointingly) as discussions of fat, breast size, and hormones. Yet something important happened in those gatherings anyway, feelings of intimacy and respect for each other emerged—feelings that women had rarely had for each other before in their scramble to catch men. It was in these funky meetings that some insight was gained into the assumptions being made about our gender, by ourselves as much as by men, and so a refusal to collaborate was begun in living rooms and kitchens after dark.

At that time, after their father and I broke up, survival for my children and myself as their only caretaker was all that drove me. I learned how to bend the rules, to prevaricate, to be crooked, to get something for as little as nothing, to take now and pay later, to fake facts in exchange for safety, to live by smoke alone, to feel grateful to cheap wine at night, to find the free clinics, the kind people, the food stamp outlet, and to exchange free childcare with other mothers. The potential for corruption that is in all of us is certainly triggered by the feeling of being absolutely alone in a desperate situation. I would do anything for my children. The emotion was not heroic or tough even. It was reactive. When this kind of situation lasts for a while, your adaptation to crookedness can alter your personality unless you watch out. There is a point when you realize you are spending more time covering the traces of your dishonesty than you spend plotting it. I know women now, I recognize them, who are powerful and lively spirits, who have nonetheless become permanently dishonest in response to several difficult years caring for their children alone. I know that they would lie to their own best friends to get an extra buck, years after the need for that was over.

(The problem with this kind of survival ethic when you are parenting is that the results of a well-intended action only show up years later. At the time, in the nearsightedness of desperate acts, you may be aspiring to goodness for all involved, you may have only unselfish motives in mind as you make decisions, but they can be wrong for one of the people. You can sacrifice a long-term good for a short-term result. Acts driven by worry unfold slowly and a long unhappiness can be the result.)

When I finally did have to strike close to the streets (we lost our house, we had no money and nowhere to go, and made daily visits to dismal welfare and food stamp offices) it was a stretch that truly scared me, but there were several women who helped me out. One of these women was a young black psychiatrist, Daryl Utz, who worked at the neighborhood clinic. She was a brilliant and gentle counselor through this time—seated in a dismal office adjacent to the giant hospitals off the Riverway in Boston—wet snow falling outside. We shared champagne at New Year's, we became friends, she told me, "You married your mother!" I started commuting to New York to work two days a week, and on one of the days at home, she called me to say, "I am going to reverse roles and cancel our appointment for today." And then she committed suicide. It was this tragedy that gave me the impetus to leave Boston and settle in a shack in the woods in Connecticut. I saw Boston as a prison then, a race nightmare. Her isolated home in a white suburban tract where she had died seemed to be a metaphor for no-place-to-run-no-place-to-hide.

Nevertheless I, like her, chose the country, a wood by the sea, to recover in: a small town with a kind day care staff and sliding scale; a very good public school in a huge green field; my sister; and a train to New York, where I was then teaching at Columbia. The poet Maureen Owen was living in the same town and also working in New York, and we helped each other with child care when we had to spend nights away. She published two of my books of poems written at that time; we mimeoed and stapled them out in her barn. The smell of the sea and birdsongs in many ways worked as a tonic. But the race issue was a plague and a problem for the children, who had no friends of color to speak of in that small privileged town. And we were not used to living alone. We always lived with other people.

+ + +

Not for the first or last time, we were asked to leave the shack after a year (too many children; I had lied and said I only had two) and we moved into a house near the village green called The Welfare House by the neighbors. There we lived over a single mother, a Korean woman named Kyong, with her son Michael, and we became an extended family happily. It was the mid-seventies. We were then a family of four living on $6,000 a year, my income from adjunct teaching at Columbia. A small town is far preferable on a daily basis to a city when you are poor, but the catch-22 is that there are few opportunities for work, for changing your situation. You can comfortably squat in the same economic position there for many years. I felt stagnant and lacking in hope there.

With my return, then, to Boston, in search of more opportunity, I began to play the school system, along with many other single mothers, moving from one part of the city to the other following the zoning. Racialization of our children began immediately—they were coded by hair and skin tone to travel to one or another school, sometimes different ones. I remember fighting out this issue with an official over a table in some school in West Roxbury, until we found a school all three children could attend together. This perverse operation taught me to use race in my children's favor, calling them black in one district and white in another, in order to get the good school. I wrote an article for the *Boston Globe* at that time called "The Nouveau Pauvre" describing my own situation, as someone from the middle class who had fallen below the poverty line with droves of others, mostly women, and how we coped with it. We formed food coops and community gardens in abandoned lots running along the tracks to downtown Boston. And we also learned how to entangle the issues of economics and race in ways that served our children's interests.

Having determined that our children would get the kind of education that we had had, but having no money to support that determination, we not only taught them at home, we also tracked them for Boston Latin, the city's best public school, or Brookline High School, as soon as we had steered them through the maze of Boston's elementary-school system during the busing crisis. Whites were abandoning Boston for the suburbs, where the busing order was not enforced, in order to avoid sending their children to school with black children, and they left behind a trail of scrawled messages: *Nigger Go Home*. And some of those same whites worked in the city and often liberally encouraged poor whites and blacks to continue their struggle for integrated schools. It was the well-known American story: at all costs, don't mention economic injustice. Increasingly race was a red herring, a way to avoid seeing the ever-widening gap between rich and poor.

By the time my children were approaching sixth grade, one thing was clear: elementary school accomplishes eighty percent of the task of educating children for their entire lives. In the Boston public schools, between first and fifth grades, my children got all the basic learning they needed from excellent and committed teachers. Anything extra was my responsibility at home. From sixth grade on, the issues changed, and the school day was more of a social than an educational reality. The main lesson: learn your place in the pecking order through sports and clubs. The kids got a little history and English, bad foreign language instruction, and small science. I could be of less and less actual help, because their attention was drawn elsewhere, towards the purely social. The truth is, from middle school to graduation, the public school system was cousin to the penal system, a way of keeping unruly kids off the streets so they wouldn't disturb the grownups.

I had returned to Boston with the hope of reconstructing my marriage, but our struggles continued after we returned to live in Jamaica Plain. We had moved when once again I was asked to leave an apartment, after Kyong and Michael moved in with us, putting six people in a two-bedroom space. It was then that my cousin Quincy gave me a down payment on a big old house, and we could rent out sections of the house and in this way pay the mortgage. I also began work on a project that would take eighteen months—*The White Slave*—a novel based on the true story of a white boy raised as a slave before, during, and after the Civil War. I was paid enough by Avon to live for those months, while I looked for another teaching job and rented out rooms in the house.

I think for that time my involvement in the domestic scene formed my position in the larger world. These household ideals—which are of course social ideals too—of an extended family that lives together, sharing and helping and not competing with each other—were incompatible with an individualist approach to the social and professional arena. Between my domestic socialism and the outside world's social realism I could only construct a narrow and weak psychological bridge, one that I was finally too suspicious to cross.

+ + +

During these school-choice crises, people used false addresses, moved, and begged in order to get their kids into decent places. We kept three such students, friends of my children, listed under our address and several times had to rush to round them up before they were caught not living there. My daughters remained in Boston public schools until they went to college, and their education became the motive force behind where we could live. My son went to a private school that generously paid almost his entire fee; I sent him there so that he could have more attention than I could give him, now that I was working more hours and he had no father at home. And by the time he was six I had figured out that he was a school-hater (as I had been) and that I could place him in safe custody among generous liberals who were comfortable with his combination of familiar manners and color. The kindness of many now-despised liberals during this period was paramount in making it possible for numbers of school-age children to escape the public school system. During these years—between 1978 and 1987—there were 20,315 black males murdered in America; in 1995 alone, there were 7,913 deaths. Many of these were black-on-black murder-suicides. Most victims were children, most of them "mixed" through history.

It wasn't until five years after my divorce, when I joined those ranks of single white mothers, that I converted to Catholicism. I would have to say that my children led me to that place because I learned everything I ever hoped to learn about consequence from giving birth to them, from raising them, and from saying goodbye to them as they entered their generation's world.

THE WEDDING DRESS

I want to run through the world
And live the life of a lost child
I have caught the mood of a wandering soul
After scattering all my goods.
It is one to me whether I live or die.
All I ask is for love to remain with me.

Joseph Surin, S.J.

BEWILDERMENT

What I have been thinking about, lately, is bewilderment as a way of entering the day as much as the work.

Bewilderment as a poetics and a politics.

I have developed this idea from living in the world and also through testing it out in my poems and through the characters in my fiction—women and children, and even the occasional man, who rushed backwards and forwards within an irreconcilable set of imperatives.

What sent them running was a double bind established in childhood, or a sudden confrontation with evil in the world—that is, in themselves—when they were older, yet unprepared.

These characters remained as uncertain in the end as they were in the beginning, though both author and reader could place them within a pattern of causalities.

In their story they were unable to handle the complexities of the world or the shock of making a difference. In fact, to make a difference was to be inherently compromised. From their author's point of view the shape and form of their stories were responses to events long past, maybe even forgotten.

Increasingly my stories joined my poems in their methods of sequencing and counting. Effects can never change what made them, but they can't stop trying to.

Like a scroll or a comic book that shows the same exact character in multiple points and situations, the look of the daily world was governed only by which point you happened to be focused on at a particular time. Everything was occurring at once. So what if the globe is round? The manifest reality is flat.

There is a Muslim prayer that says, "Lord, increase my bewilderment," and this prayer belongs both to me and to the strange Whoever who goes under the name of "I" in my poems—and under multiple names in my fiction—where error, errancy, and bewilderment are the main forces that signal a story.

A signal does not necessarily mean that you want to be located or described. It can mean that you want to be known as Unlocatable and Hidden. This contradiction can drive the "I" in the lyrical poem into a series of techniques that are the reverse of the usual narrative movements around courage, discipline, conquest, and fame.

Instead, weakness, fluidity, concealment, and solitude assume their place in a kind of dream world, where the sleeping witness finally feels safe enough to lie down in mystery. These qualities are not the usual stuff of stories of initiation and success, but they may survive more than they are given credit for. They have the endurance of tramps who travel light, discarding acquisitions like water drops off a dog.

It is to the dream model that I return as a writer involved in the problem of sequencing events and thoughts—because in the weirdness of dreaming there is a dimension of plot, but a greater consciousness of randomness and uncertainty as the basic stock in which it is brewed.

Too clever a reading of a dream, too serious a closure given to its subject, the more disappointing the dream becomes in retrospect. If the dream's curious activities are subjected to an excess of inter-pretation, they are better forgotten. The same demystification can happen with the close reading of a text; sometimes a surface reading seems to bring you closer to the intention of the poem.

Sustaining a balance between the necessity associated with plot and the blindness associated with experience—in both poetry and fiction—is the trick for me. Dreams are constantly reassur-ing happenings that illuminate methods for pulling this off.

Recently I had this dream, which I will title *The Dream of Two Mothers*.

Two very old women—both of them mothers of actual friends named John and both of whom in real life have died—were in front of me simultaneously, and they were identical in appearance.

One represented the public (known) life, and the other the private (hidden) life. I knew this by their actions in the dream.

We were in a church basement and I said to someone beside me, "Enlightened yogis can see the aura trailing a person—it's a whole other version of the person, and sometimes I can see it too."

And as if to prove it, at that moment, someone all in red, even his flesh, drifted past us, splitting into sections, each one whole, as he moved.

His coloring was familiar to me because I knew about the red flush on the face of Moses and I had a feeling that Christ, reincarnated, was red too, and in many ikons there is a fiery red light surrounding the figures.

Red was the right color for this event and at the time I was even writing about it.

(In the dream, by then, I was conscious that I was in a dream and that I must pay attention.)

The man, now a priest, drifted upstairs with his multiple selves following to prepare for mass, and I waited with the old women, where I had time to ponder the strange question of these two old mothers who in the dream were identical, though not at all so in life.

One woman might as well have been called Way Out There and the other one Way Inside, because one was rushing around doing things as a mediator, mother, Martha, and martyr for the other one who was still and pensive.

I could see, as increasingly nothing began to happen in the dream, that Way Inside could not exist without Way Out There—they were bound to the point that each was a different embodiment of the same actual human.

They were splitting and re-forming into one and the other, as birds can sometimes seem to do, whole flocks of the same shape bursting up into the sky.

And though it was not quite the end of the dream, these images at its center haunted me as if it had been a revelation.

While I can see that the Witness I (who perhaps could be called Q) in the dream expressed the bewilderment for which the Muslim of the prayer was praying for more of, the dream also illuminated a method for describing sequential persons, first and third.

As we all know, a dream hesitates, it doesn't grasp, it stands back, it jokes, it makes itself scared, it circles, and it fizzles.

A dream often undermines the narratives of power and winning. It is instead dazzled and horrified.

The dreamer is aware that only everything else but this tiny dream exists and in this way the dream itself is free to act without restraint.

A dream breaks into parts and contradicts its own will, even as it travels around and around.

For me, bewilderment is like a dream: one continually returning pause on a gyre and in both my stories and my poems it could be the shape of the spiral that imprints itself in my interior before anything emerges on paper.

For to the spiral-walker there is no plain path, no up and down, no inside or outside. But there are strange returns and recognitions and never a conclusion.

What goes in, goes out. Just as a well-known street or house forms a living and expressive face that looks back at you, so do all the weirdly familiar bends in the spiral.

The being both inside and outside simultaneously of the world is not just a writer's problem by any means.

To start the problem over again:

What I have recently noticed is that there is a field of faith that the faithful inhabit.

If you choose to enter this field after them, you enter questioning and you endlessly seek a way to explain and defend your choice to be there.

When you remain outside the field, you see that it requires no explanation or defense.

You, on the outside, perhaps better than those always inhabiting the field, know that it doesn't matter whether you are inside or outside the faith-field, because there is no inside or outside anyway under an undiscriminating sky. The atheist is no less an inquirer than a believer. In living at all, she is no less a believer than an unbeliever.

God's mercy can often seem too close to neutrality for comfort.

As Beckett has written in *Watt:* ". . . now the western sky was as the eastern, which was as the southern, which was as the northern."

Into such boundless perplexity King Midas—following his wish to have everything he touched turn to gold—wandered. Now he touched, but touched without receiving a response, only a hardening.

I remember that when I read this story as a child I already knew that there was a thin coating of gold on all objects. Whether the light was from the sun, or from an artificial bulb, there was always gold filtering over everything. So when I read about Midas touching his daughter, their roses, the water in the fountain, and the servants—and watching each one go solid—I felt that the potential had been there all along. It was frightening to realize that a simple wish could conjure up a surface reality and fix it to the roots. The lesson seemed to involve more than greed—it was about looking too hard and too possessively at living things.

The formation of his unhappiness lay in inhabiting an unresponsive world.

The hours he wandered through his gardens, among the leaden flowers, was he asking if he was really the author of all this? Can you wish a new world into being? And when he found that his child was a gold statue, while he remained free and sensitive, he must have been repulsed by his own hand. The usual interludes between fixed matter and a change in conditions were condensed into a spread of sameness.

He wouldn't ever again have to wonder: Where *is* the future?

He could now plan his future down to the smallest detail, which is really the definition of an anti-creation story.

In terms of bewilderment and poetics, the Midas story is a story that goes right to the heart of a purely materialist and skeptical position and shows the inherent error in it. The single-minded passion that drove Midas to wish that everything he touched would turn to gold ends with this question:

How could he survive on gold nuggets for supper?

Who would love him?

However I can't really talk about bewilderment as a poetics and an ethics without first recollecting the two fundamental and oppositional life-views that coexist in many of us. That is, the materialist-skeptical view and the invisible-faithful view.

Many of us know only too well the first one—we live it.

According to some Sufis, it was God's loneliness and desire to be known that set creation going. Unmanifest things, lacking names, remained unmanifest until the violence of God's sense of isolation sent the heavens into a spasm of procreating words that then became matter.

God was nowhere until it was present to itself as the embodied names of animals, minerals, and vegetables.

On the day of creation Divine transcendence was such an emotional force, energy coalesced into these forms and words.

Now the One who wanted to be known dwells in the hearts of humans who carry the pulse of the One's own wanting to be known by the ones who want in return to be known by it.

Lacking is in this case expressed by the presence of something—the longing to be loved—and so humanity, composed of this longing, misses the very quality that inhabits itself.

Ordinary problems of logic like: Where were you before you got here? How did you arrive before my eyes?—foment in the background of this creation story.

Just as language evolves with increasing specificity, breaking further and further into qualifying parts, so words, as weak as birds, survive because they move collectively and restlessly, as if under siege.

This is at the root of the incarnational experience of being— that one is inhabited by the witness who is oneself and by that witness's creator simultaneously.

The question is, what is it to be familiar? (Why am I familiar to myself at all? Or is it my self that is familiar to some inhabitant behind my existence?)

The mystery of thought can only be solved by thought itself— which is what?

Martin Buber has written, "Every name is a step toward the consummate Name, as everything broken points to the unbroken." The awareness of both continuum and rupture occurring together may form the very rhythm of consciousness.

To the Sufis, words precede existence, perhaps because a cry brings people running.

Using a small grammatical ploy, the poet and philosopher Ibn Arabi reveals the overlap between the caller and the called when he writes that the Spirit wanted "to reveal, to it, through it, its mystery."

One "it" is not distinguished from another "it" by a capital I, or by quotes, or by calling "it" "itself"—as in "the Spirit wanted to reveal itself through its mystery."

Instead the sentence is deliberately constructed so that the Divine It and its "it" are indistinguishable and confusing.

In the Psalms the oscillation between You and He in one verse that refers only to the Lord in both cases may also be a syntactical method for dealing with simultaneity of a Way Out There and a Way Inside. But it is destabilizing.

In Sufi poetry, between the Divine seeing itself in the things of creation and sentient beings seeing the Divine in themselves, there is a constant oscillation and clearing and darkening.

Time is not a progression but something more warped and refractive.

Language, as we have it, fails to deal with confusion.

People fear repeating one word in the same sentence. They pause to avoid it every time, almost superstitiously.

There is for instance no way to express actions occurring simultaneously without repeating all the words twice or piling the letters on top of each other. The dream of coming on new grammatical structures, a new alphabet, even a new way of reading, goes on—almost as a way to create a new human. One who could fly and jump at the same moment.

But we don't even know if Paradise is behind or ahead of us.

I can keep *un*saying what I have said, and amending it, but I can't escape the law of the words in a sentence that insists on tenses and words like "later" and "before."

So it is with this language problem that bewilderment begins to form, for me, more than an attitude—but an actual approach, a way—to settle with the unresolvable.

In the dictionary, to bewilder is "to cause to lose one's sense of where one is."

The wilderness as metaphor is in this case not evocative enough because causing a complete failure in the magnet, the compass, the scale, the stars, and the movement of the rivers is more catastrophic than getting lost in the woods.

Bewilderment is an enchantment that follows a complete collapse of reference and reconcilability.

It breaks open the lock of dualism *(it's this or that)* and peers out into space *(not this, not that)*.

The old debate over beauty—between absolute and relative—is ruined by this experience of being completely lost! Between God and No-God, between Way Out There and Way Inside—while they are vacillating wildly, there is no fixed position.

The construction of high-hedged mazes is a concession to bewilderment, just as Robert Smithson's spiral jetty rises and sinks under the weight of Utah's salt water—both site and non-site—a shape that must turn back or drop off—that can climb and wind down—that has noetic as well as poetic attributes, miming infinity in its uncertain end.

The maze and the spiral have aesthetic value since they are constructed for others—places to learn about perplexity and loss of bearing.

And even if it is associated with childhood, madness, stupidity, and failure, even if it shows not only how to get lost but also how it feels not to return, bewilderment has a high status in several mystical traditions.

+ + +

When someone is incapable of telling you the truth, when there is no certain way to go, when you are caught in a double bind, bewilderment—which, because of its root meaning—will never lead you back to common sense, but will offer you a walk into a further wild place on "the threshold of love's sanctuary which lies above that of reason."

> The summer's flower is to the summer sweet
> Though to itself it only live and die.

This walk into the wilderness is full of falls and stumbles and pains. Strangely one tries to get in deeper and to get home at the same time. There is a sense of repetition and unfamiliarity being in collusion.

Each bruise on you is like the difference between a signature semiconsciously scrawled across a page and a forgery deliberately and systematically copied by a person who stops and watches her own hand producing shapes.

The forgery has more contour, more weight. In its effort to seem real, it cuts deeper into the paper and the fingers.

A liar can reproduce the feeling that a wilderness does.

In Sufism "the pupil of the eye" is the owner of each member of the body, even the heart, and each part becomes a tool under its lens. It is in and through and with the pupil of the eye that the catch locks between just-being and always-being. The less focused the gesture, the more true to the eye of the heart it is.

You are progressing at one level and becoming more lost at another.

The owner of the eye is the Divine Non-Existent about whom one can only speculate.

At certain points, wandering around lost produces the (perhaps false) impression that events approach you from ahead, that time is moving backwards onto you, and that the whole scenario is operating in reverse from the way it is ordinarily perceived.

You may have the impression that time is repeating with only slight variations, because here you are again!

Each movement forwards is actually a catching of what is coming at you, as if someone you are facing across a field has thrown a ball and stands watching you catch it.

Watching and catching combine as a forward action that has come from ahead.

All intention then is reversed into attention.

Mentally, an effect precedes its cause because the whole event needs to unravel in order for it all to be interpreted.

The serial poem attempts to demonstrate this attention to what is cyclical, returning, but empty at its axis. To me, the serial poem is a spiral poem.

In this poetry circling can take form as sublimations, inversions, echolalia, digressions, glossolalia, and rhymes.

An aesthetic that organizes its subject around a set of interlocking symbols and metaphors describes a world that is fixed and fatally subject to itself alone.

Decorating and perfecting any subject can be a way of removing all stench of the real until it becomes an astral corpse.

+ + +

In an itinerant and disposable work each event is greeted as an alternative, either the equivalent of respite or a way out.

Space may only indicate something else going on, somewhere else, all that lies beyond perceptions.

There is a new relationship to time and narrative, when the approach through events and observations is not sequential but dizzying and repetitive. The dance of the dervish is all about this experience.

> Since the upright man is kin to the stumbling drunk
> to whose sultry glance should we give our heart? What is
>   choice?
> — *Hafiz*

The whirling that is central to bewilderment is the natural way for the lyric poet. A dissolving of particularities into one solid braid of sound is her inspiration.

Each poem is a different take on an idea, an experience, each poem is another day, another mood, another revelation, another conversion.

> A void was made in Nature; all her bonds
> Cracked; and I saw the flaring atom-streams
> And torrents of her myriad universe
> Running along the illimitable inane.
> — *Tennyson*

What Shelley called "the One Spirit's plastic stress" and Hopkins called "instress" is this matching up of the outwardly observed with the internally heard.

A call and response to and from a stranger is implied.

Or a polishing of a looking glass where someone is looking in and out at the same time.

Particularities are crushed and compacted and redesigned to produce a new sound.

The new sound has muted the specific meanings of each word and a perplexing music follows.

Themes of pilgrimage of an unrequited love, of wounding and seeking come up a lot in this tradition.

Every experience that is personal is simultaneously an experience that is supernatural.

How you love another person might be a reflection of your relationship to God or the world itself, not to the other person, not to any other person, mother, father, sister, brother. Untrusting? Suspicious? Jealous? Indifferent? Abject? These feelings may be an indication of your larger existential position, hardly personal.

And the heart is an organ of the soul, in such a case, not the reverse.

In your cyclical movements you often have to separate from situations and people you love, and the more you love them the more difficult it is to allow anyone new to replace them.

This action can produce guilt, withdrawal, and rumination that some might read as depression. But to preserve, and return to a past you have voluntarily left—to suffer remorse—has always signaled a station in spiritual progress.

The human heart, transforming on a seventy-two-hour basis (the Muslim measurement of a day in relation to conversion of faith and conduct) in a state of bewilderment, doesn't want to answer questions so much as to lengthen the resonance of those questions.

Bewilderment circumnavigates, believing that at the center of errant or circular movement is the empty but ultimate referent.

> Shall I compare thee to a summer's day?
> Thou art more lovely and more temperate.
> Rough winds do shake the darling buds of May
> and summer's lease hath all too short a date.
> — *Shakespeare*

For poets, the obliquity of a bewildered poetry is its own theme.

Q—the Quidam, Whoever, the unknown one—or I, is turning in a circle and keeps passing herself on her way around, her former self, her later self, and the trace of this passage is marked by a rhyme, a coded message for "I have been here before, I will return."

The same sound splays the sound waves into a polyvalence, a rose. A bloom is not a parade.

A big error comes when you believe that a form, name, or position in which the subject is viewed is the only way that the subject can be viewed. This is called "binding" and it leads directly to painful contradiction and clashes. It leads to war in the larger world.

No monolithic answers that are not soon disproved are allowed into a bewildered poetry or life.

According to a Kabbalistic rabbi, in the Messianic age people will no longer quarrel with others but only with themselves.

This is what poets are doing already.

"A thing of beauty is a joy forever," wrote Keats in the first line of *Endymion* and then hundreds of lines followed wrestling with the problems surrounding this grandiose statement.

The line, probably dictated to him in the Spicer sense, presented him with a hard subject, and he had to see if it carried through.

He circled it, pouring out sound-relations and image-associations that put it to the test of a true bewilderment, building an integrated system that turned, like the uroborus, back on itself.

The poem's last line is, "Peona went home through the gloomy wood in wonderment."

It is a very long lyrical poem. The stanzas are very long too.

Now we have lyrical poems that are written as fully wrought integrated units that include tiny stanzas and a lot of space.

One definition of the lyric might be that it is a method of searching for something that can't be found. It is an air that blows and buoys and settles. It says, "Not this, not this," instead of , "I have it."

Sequences of lyrical poems have the heave, thrill, and murmur of the nomadic heart. Though they may at first look like static, fixed-place poems with a confessional personal base, they hold the narrator up as an idea, even an abstract example, of consciousness shifting in its spatial locations.

The same was true of early Celtic poetry that never went as high as myth, but never went as low as the purely personal, in describing the harrowing nature of pilgrimage.

As in Sufi poetry, in these short and long lyrical works there is a wide swing between experience and transcendence—the author is at one level empty of personality, a limited observer of his own isolation, and at another he is awake and interpreting.

> The sealight where you float,
> The glint from lifting oars,
> Are also solid earth,
> Moulded yellow and blue.
>
> You see speckled salmon
> Flash from the white sea's womb:
> They are calves, fleecy lambs
> Living in peace, not war.

These lines come from an eighth-century poem called "The Double Vision of Manannan."

The illuminati used flagellation, levitation, and starvation as a method of accounting for the power of the invisible world over their lives. Public suffering and scars gave the evidence of hidden miseries that had begun to require daylight and an audience.

The politics of bewilderment belongs only to those who have little or no access to an audience or a government. It involves circling the facts, seeing the problem from varying directions, showing the weaknesses from the bottom up, the conspiracies, the lies, the plans, the false rhetoric; the politics of bewilderment runs against myth, or fixing, binding, and defending. It's a politics devoted to the little and the weak; it is grassroots in that it imitates the way grass bends and springs back when it is stepped on. It won't go away but will continue asking irritating questions to which it knows all the answers.

After all, the point of art—like war—is to show people that life is worth living by showing that it isn't.

FAIRIES

Everything I know about fairies comes from Oscar Wilde's mother, Francesca Speranza—or Lady Wilde. She wrote *Legends of Ancient Ireland*, which was published in England in 1902. She gathered her evidence from "oral communications with the peasantry" and from history texts where she begins:

"From the beautiful Eden-land at the head of the Persian Gulf, where creeds and cultures rose to life, the first migrations emanated," including flocks of fairies traveling from Iran to Erin.

Of those fairies—the *Sidhe* of Ireland—she writes, "Their voices were heard in the mountain echo, and their forms seen in the purple and golden mountain mist; they whispered amidst the perfumed hawthorn branches; the rush of the autumn leaves was the scamper of little elves—red, yellow, and brown—wind-elven, and dancing in their glee; and the bending of the waving barley was caused by the flight of the Elf King and his Court across the fields. They danced with soundless feet, and their step was so light that the drops of dew they danced on only trembled but did not break."

Lady Wilde's collection of Irish folklore has as its primary sources Christianity and Sublime Pantheism, but, once in motion, the volume becomes a story book, a collection of herbal medicines, an account of the saints and their eccentricities and of Fakirs (the sacred fraternity of beggars), and a discussion of antiquities and early Irish art.

It is a learned book, written with respect, humor, and curiosity. One would not mind being stuck with it, and it alone, for a year or so. Fairies are described as fallen angels, but not birds who are the angels' angels, according to Dante, but ones who descended from paradise.

Fairies are powerful and to this day many people won't tamper with their rings on the drumlins. Now how did fairy tales come to be called fairy tales, since they often have nothing to do with fairies? One thought is that fairies themselves whispered these stories into kitchens and beds around the world. The pantheistic, the pagan, the petrifying truths conveyed in fairy tales do have something resonant of a world that recently included paradise. (Read Edmund Spenser's *Faery Queen*.) No need for an afterlife in such a glorious world. Paradise is the earth and our air a holy halo around it. Or else: this *is* the afterlife, the trace and effect of every gesture that comes before the one being made right now.

"The bending of the waving barley was caused by the flight of the Elf King and his Court across the fields."

+ + +

According to Lady Wilde, the *Feadh-Ree* (fairy) is a riff on the word *Peri*, the Persian mystic race that flew about the Gulf invisibly. They live in a land of perpetual youth, but are fated to perish utterly on Chastisement Day. They drink nectar from flowers and wear their yellow hair long to the ground. They have too much pride and their population exceeds ours. Many fairy stories are about babies, lovers, dying people and their corpses, those liminal happenings effected by spells and fairy music.

Fairies love music, for one thing, so if things are going badly for you, play some music and the fairies will be enamored of the sound and forget their naughty business. They especially love to dance on May Day when they mimic the two circle revolutions of sun and moon. If you put your ear to the ground, you can hear fairy-music, believe it or not. Approaching a dolmen in some wild meadow in Ireland, don't get confused by how small the door is leading inside, because humans were much smaller in stature in Megalithic times. The true "little people" dig holes in the ground, like gophers, and use snapdragons for crockery.

When I was a child in Killiney, south of Dublin, I saw a fairy on a stone wall—a tiny man in green and brown—but my mother, close by, didn't see him or believe me. We were on our way to visit the Druid chair that faces the rising sun under some sacred oak trees (now encircled by suburban housing, but left alone) to make parting wishes before our return to America. Years later, my son—a boy drunk on too much reading in *The Crock of Gold* and *The Gnome Book*—swore that he saw elves gallivanting in a field in Stonington, Connecticut.

I myself have always been gullible. Consequently my life is errant and my stories are a defense of mistaken beliefs. I am skeptical before convinced believers and become cruel when they get too sure of themselves. When people write for children, they must defend belief, but it is harder to do so when you are writing for adults.

Lady Wilde writes, "The Leprechauns are merry, industrious, tricky little sprites, who do all the shoemaker's work and the tailor's and the cobbler's for the fairy gentry, and are often seen at sunset under the hedge singing and stitching." It is the littleness of these creatures that puts them deep into nature, not as spirits of nature, but as sentient participants in foliage and riverbend. While Thoreau was leaning over his windowsill watching the war of the red ants versus the black, it was only his imagination that could interpret their little activities a posteriori. But Lady Wilde seemed to have had experience with leprechauns when she wrote that they can twist a shoe into a shape under a dock leaf. Tininess and handiwork go together. Still, fairies can also cure a sick cow and cut paths through human houses because they change form, size, and intention at will.

William Blake described seeing the following in his garden in Sussex: "There was a great stillness among the branches and flowers, and more than common sweetness in the air; I heard a low and pleasant sound and I knew not whence it came. At last I saw the broad leaf of a flower move, and underneath I saw a procession of creatures, of the color and size of green and grey grasshoppers, bearing a body laid out on a rose-leaf, which they buried with songs, and then disappeared. It was a fairy funeral."

Lady Wilde was Anglo-Irish. Her family came from Wexford. She had masses of hair, was very large, and she named herself Speranza. She was a major intellectual figure in Dublin and was devoted to her son Oscar through his trials just as she stood by her husband through his trial for rape. She was relentless in her loyalties and in her research into Irish folklore. She was superstitious and, though a Protestant, a lover of Catholicism. My own mother is Anglo-Irish, her paternal family dating back to the sixteenth century, from County Kerry, and from a long line of crooked men, but the women in her family like Speranza were often political activists, nationalists, and scholars. When we were children my mother played a record of Orson Welles (who had studied with her at the Gate Theater in Dublin) reading "The Happy Prince" by Oscar Wilde.

This reading—set to music—reduced us all to tears every time, and remains with me as one of the most spell-binding fairy tales ever written. Far more in the tradition of Hans Christian Andersen than Grimm, one feels deeply the links between the Celtic imagination and the Scandinavian in this sorrowful story of altruism. Orson Welles—as artificial in much of his "theater" as Wilde was in his life—read the story in melodious, deep-throated tones: "Swallow, swallow, little swallow, will you not stay with me one night longer?" In the story the good ones die and the vain and foolish survive as philistines of progress. But as with Andersen, Wilde's story ends on a Christian note—written and uttered with such genuine belief that the story did establish a little theological hope.

In Michael MacLiammoir's introduction to Wilde's fairy tales, he writes that Wilde's "son Vyvyan Holland tells us how, when his father was tired of playing with him and his brother Cyril, he would keep them quiet by telling them fairy stories. 'There was one,' Mr. Holland says, 'about the fairies who lived in the great bottles of coloured water that the chemists used to put in their windows, with lights behind them that made them take on all kinds of different shapes. The fairies came down from their bottles at night and played and danced and made pills in the empty shop. Cyril once asked him why his father had tears in his eyes when he told us the story of the Selfish Giant, and he replied that 'really beautiful things always made him cry.'"

At the end of "The Happy Prince" he wrote (and must have been weeping when he wrote it):

> "Bring me the two most precious things in the city," said
> God to one of His Angels; and the Angel brought Him the
> leaden heart and the dead bird.
>   "You have rightly chosen," said God, "for in my garden
> of Paradise this little bird shall sing for evermore, and in my
> city of gold the Happy Prince shall praise me."

Wilde also wrote a longer story called "The Fisherman and His Soul," which tells the story of a handsome young fisherman who sells his soul for the love of a mermaid. He does so despite the warnings of a priest: "Accursed be the Fauns of the woodland, and accursed be the singers of the sea! I have seen them at night-time, and they have sought to lure me from my beads. They tap at the window and laugh. They whisper into my ears the tale of their perilous joys. They tempt me with temptations, and when I would pray they make mouths at me. They are lost, I tell thee, they are lost. For them there is no heaven nor hell, and in neither shall they praise God's name." This tale concerns itself less with the fisherman than with the experience of his soul—void of a heart—roaming the earth. Immoral, voyeuristic, this shadow (like the shadow-soul in Hans Christian Andersen's tales) becomes a Satanic spirit. The fisherman, on the other hand, is absolved ultimately of sin because of the purity of his love for the mermaid. This fairy tale, read in the light of Wilde's personal life, and his last prose work—*De Profundis*—prefigures his more "out" contemporary fairy tales. ("To deny one's own experiences is to put a lie into the lips of one's own life. It's no less than a denial of the soul.")

Something about time is involved in the existence of fairies: the way time runs ahead of us, while we seem, as humans, to be discarded by a future that is chasing us in the form of the past. Into all of this drops the tale. In fact the controlling mechanism at work in writing—that is, the effort at stabilizing time, of imprinting little figures on sheets of paper and packing them tight—is similar to the pretend games children play. Toy soldiers, dollhouses, "the world of counterpane"—this is activity that generates fiction. The writer (like the child) is hunched over the page, controlling little signs and symbols that replicate, imaginatively, a population he or she is manipulating. The characters look back, helpless, dismayed, to no avail.

An Austrian writer from the mid-nineteenth century, Adalbert Stifter, wrote a collection of stories called *Colored Stones;* some are ecstatic depictions of mountains and the children who inhabit them. One story, especially, called "Rock Crystal," and translated into English by Marianne Moore, is a fairy tale that exists in a real place and time. (Not in a "once-upon-a-time" as in "hovering over" transcendentally.) This is a real mountain village that the author has known, yet the story is laden with the pantheism of the true fairy tale. Correspondences between the soul and the earth are carefully, painstakingly "painted in words" by Stifter in this great novella.

One Christmas Eve two children—a brother and sister (a relationship that is ideal because it is both inclusive and "without sin," and suggests the possibilities of a new kind of partnership based in love-without-greed)—are sent out through a mountain pass to visit their grandmother. She lives in a village that is in many ways "alien" from the one her daughter has married into. On their way home the children become lost in a snowstorm in the mountains (or lost in a description of a snowstorm in the mountains), take shelter in an icy chasm overnight, and in the night sky before dawn, when it seems sure that they will die of cold, this is what they see:

"The children sat, open-eyed, gazing up at the small stars. Something now began to happen as they watched. While they sat thus, a faint light bloomed amid the stars, describing upon the heavens a delicate arc. The faint green luminescence traveled slowly downward. But the arc grew brighter and brighter until the stars paled away, while a shudder of light, invading other parts of the firmament—taking on an emerald tinge—vibrated and flooded the stellar spaces. Then from the highest point of the arc sheaves radiated like points of a crown, all aglow. Adjacent horizons caught the brightening flush; it flickered and spread in faint quivers through the vastness around about. . . ." Stifter then suggests the scientific explanation for this, but then lets it go, and in minute detail describes the fading of the phenomenon and its replacement by daybreak.

Partly because of the Grimm echoes in the story of a brother and sister becoming lost, but also because of the spirit-nature of the mountains themselves, this story can be seen as a variation on a fairy tale. However, unlike Wilde's religious ending, Stifter's conclusion, as in all his stories, is an absolutely cold one. The children's rescue and return to their village is a triumph of communal human effort, a reaffirmation of the importance of national identity. They have erred and been set right again. The social issue is in the end the subject of the story, but it is suffused with ambivalence and irony. While there are no fairies in Stifter's stories, the fleeting figure of hope ("cosmic love") is drawn in the night skies, a hope that is liberated from cause and effect. As in the story of Pandora, where hope is released from their treasure-box with all the sins of the world, Stifter in his fine, odd stories lets us know everything else is there, too, including prejudiced villagers and a grandmother whose love is "morbid."

The British-Guyanese writer Wilson Harris has written:

"The frame that conventional realism uses endorses the absence of cosmic love. It consolidates the nation-state and the vested interests of the nation-state."

This story by Stifter endorses cosmic love and yet it proves the fleeting nature of that love in the face of the civilized world.

A contemporary and much more sorrowful version of the same story is the film *Landscape in the Mist* by Theo Angelopoulos. Again, two children—a brother and sister—set off by themselves and become lost. They are searching for their father, who they have been told abandoned them and went to Germany. Dismal train rides, lonely highways, urban squalor, and cruelty—all these become allegorical stations in their search for the mythical father.

The film is short on speech, but poetic when voices do emerge, and the ecstatic ending of the film—a vision redolent of Paradise—brings one face-to-face with the tenacity of hope in the midst of a poisoned landscape. The soft children's voice-overs become little haunts from a fairy-haunted past.

Once, when I was nervous beyond belief, I pretended that all the people on the street were elves, and what had before looked like a mass of huge mechanical insects now was reduced to a cheerful mob of little people. I felt much better. However there is no lasting escape from the reality of malign powers that drive us all along. While that fantasy got me home safely on the bus, its use-value would soon grow weak.

+ + +

Fairies explain as well as anything else the way we feel about the arrival of suffering, sickness, and obstacles seemingly out of nowhere.

Lady Wilde wrote: "A farmer[,] who had lost one son by heart disease (always a mysterious malady to the peasants) and another by gradual decay, consulted a wise fairy woman as to what should be done, for his wife also had become delicate and weak. The woman told him that on November Eve the fairies had made a road through the house, and were going back and forward ever since, and whatever they looked upon was doomed. The only remedy was to build up the old door and open another entrance. This the man did, and when the witch-women came as usual in the morning to beg for water or milk or meal they found no door, and were obliged to turn back. After this the spell was taken off the household, and they all prospered without fear of the fairies."

Speranza Wilde took the fairies' side, being herself pagan in her allegiance to a rustic and mystic earth with blowing red and yellow leaves, clear blue waters, herbs and potions for cures, and stories to explain them. Speranza's learning, her love of Ireland, obviously nurtured her son's enduring interest in an earth populated by aliens (fairies, giants, angels). We all have the potential for flight to these airy regions, away from the prescriptive social fictions of adults, but it is hard to revisit them without children. Do fairies come from outer space and yearn to return there? Do they wish us to write a different kind of tale—not the ones we have been told about winners and losers? Why did they enter our stories in the first place, if not to remind us of chaos?

+ + +

The story of Pinocchio is a story about fairies and mothers too.

The Blue-Haired Fairy is an alien being who stands in for Pinocchio's never-created mother.

She and the puppet pretend to have a normal mother-son relationship.

And in this game she lets her wooden boy be changed into a donkey, beaten, thrown in the ocean, hanged from a tree, and chained by the neck, and when he is swallowed finally by the whale and is of no more value to the world than a matchstick, he calls "Father! Father!" in the bubbling Disney version of the story, and is saved.

In the original book, Gepetto is a disagreeable old man who takes pleasure from Pinocchio's disasters, so the puppet has to find his own way out of that glossy fish and back into the world of indifferent adults before he can become a real boy.

But he has to perform selfless tasks before his alien mother will say to him: "Brave Pinocchio! Be good in the future and you will be happy." And then Pinocchio becomes a real boy, leaving his puppet form abandoned and looped over a chair. And the fairy evaporates into outer space.

This story or any other about a fairy or a puppet springs from an ancient unease with the animate. For instance, if antelopes can grow wooden branches out of their heads, why can't the world also produce wooden figures that move on their own, or floating insects with human faces and speech? These creatures would not be truly human of course, because they would lack reason.

So while Pinocchio has to suffer before he can be human, and while he also has to learn compassion towards his mean father, he first has to show the fairy whom he calls mother how senseless he is. When he is a puppet running between people's legs and knocking things down, cutting school and being rude to policemen, he always gets rebuked and humiliated. Since he is not yet fully human, he can be brutally punished.

He calls on his alien mother for help, but she turns a cold shoulder. She teases and tests him and only pretends to love him. She is a classic not-good-enough mother, one who plays the game of the double bind with her offspring. He has to be good in order to be loved by her but she never gives him a clue on how to be good, or what goodness means; instead he has to go through literal hell and high water himself to figure it out.

Only then does she say, "I forgive you for all your past misdeeds."

In some ways this fairy mother is not as alien as she might seem. From her point of view Pinocchio is only wood and therefore can be played with, and she can derive pleasure from watching him fail without ever having to see him die. He is her toy, her work.

She is in many ways like mothers who, when the children are small, can stay home and play, hide away from the patriarchs and judges, and let imagination roam free.

She can pretend, with them, that there is nothing really bad out there.

For a fairy mother a naughty puppet is preferable to a real child who is mortal. It can be twisted, maltreated, uprooted, deformed, and used as a scapegoat.

It can also be sent out the door to be disruptive and adventuresome, to be a rebel.

A mother gives birth to someone who won't last; she has to love someone who will leave, to teach a child who will suffer anyway how to avoid all pain. To be a mother you have to hold down a job that you can never quit.

In most mothers, there is a fairy who wants to fly free. In some it is their art that gives them wings. Its inertia is their liberty. Her bad puppet is her writing, her music, her painting, her dance, sculpture, film; it is her critique of society. Unlike her vulnerable flesh-child, her puppet is the work that she can swing from a noose, bang on the ground, stamp on, throw in the water, and send into battle against the outside world.

Her wooden artifact (book, film, painting) shoots from the nothing-air of her imagination.

This puppet is herself heroically projected.

For a mother of children the art-work is the expression of an unrealized and undefined life. It is a twin and a toy forever, always secondary in value to the animated mortal child.

Her problem comes later when she pushes the poor work out the door and into the marketplace and tries to make it "sell."

This confusion between a thing that is made out of nothing and the market economy that prices all materials is perhaps more intense for a mother than for any other. Her awareness of the supernatural is intensified daily by the cries of the natural.

She loves her child and she adores her work.

Her crisis comes at the threshold to a world where there is a terrifying cacophony of machines awaiting both her work and her children.

IMMANENCE

When I was a child I was hyperconscious of the silence surrounding all matter and at first this silence was a dynamic that encouraged me. As time went by, however, the silence became increasingly erratic in the lengths and directions of its waves and not so partial to me.

Being a child of the twentieth century I suppose that the emotional source of this fixation on silence may have come from my father's absence during the Second World War and my yearning for his return. On the other hand, my attention to what was missing may have begun earlier, when this fullness in the air vanished because it vanished the minute I welcomed it consciously.

That body of light and listening around my crib simply moved on as soon as I let it know that I knew it was there. After that it actually seemed to thicken and collaborate with the world in a larger plan for my personal isolation. I began to wonder if the negative emotional responses that emerge in a lifetime aren't generated by that first loss of stability and containment—one that precedes even the loss of security among parents and other people—because it is the loss of a feeling of enfoldment in the whole cosmos, not just in a household. It is huge, but integrating.

Over time my apprehensions came and went in three forms: the fear of God, the fear that there was an unknowable ( ), and the fear that there was no God at all. And theology became "the queen of philosophy" for me thereafter.

The story of Edith Stein helps me to see some of these apprehensions acted out in a fierce and wholehearted way, over a lifetime. Hers is the story of a skeptical Jewish philosopher who poured meaning back into the abyss, who "found God," who came to believe that Catholicism was the fulfillment of Judaism—its outcome, its offspring—and who changed her way of thinking and living during the ruthless flow of mid-twentieth-century history. Her story represents the deliberate choice of one epistemology over another as an act of self-salvation. Stein was always analytical and feminist but she became committed to finding a way to articulate the limits of knowledge, and to discover if these limits became signs of a liberating intelligence and presence that was inherent in all things and places in the world.

She was born a Prussian citizen near the end of the nineteenth century. She grew up in a large Jewish matriarchy after the premature death of her father. Her mother was a powerful and practical woman who ran her husband's business and her own household for years. Edith was her youngest, adored child. They were observant Jews, comfortably adapted to the European culture in which they worked and lived.

Edith was a clever child who had tantrums and led an intense solitary life even among her many siblings. She was an atheist early on and later became Husserl's favorite student, working with him in Freiburg, and with other students, men and women who would remain her friends for life. She was said to understand Husserl's method better than anyone, and he hired her to help him with many of his papers. She wrote her own essays too, spending hours alone in her room or at the library. She seems to have had many friends and at least one serious romantic encounter, but little has been made public about this so far.

Despite her brilliant student career, her efforts to find scholarly work afterwards were thwarted because of her being a woman and a Jew. Although she was born and trained to be a thinker and a teacher who would thrive in an academic environment, the political milieu in which she grew up conspired to prevent this. After a while she became aware that the Catholic Church had work for her and would also allow her to continue her own studies. She began rather slowly and secretly to spend her time in a church environment, around schools where even Jewish women could think and teach and publish some of their work.

Her interest in scholasticism and her disappointment with German philosophic thought seemed to develop while she was experiencing profound personal frustrations. With her time increasingly dedicated to Catholic girls' education, she developed her feminist position on women, work, and love and continued her study of Aquinas, the phenomenologist of the Middle Ages. She, like him, would come to the conclusion that the intellect was only useful while human will and faith were liberating.

She became a Catholic on January 1, 1922. Other secular Jews in her environment were doing the same thing, though many converted to Protestantism. A couple of intense personal experiences—one with the writings of Saint Teresa and another with the bereaved widow of a friend—helped move her in this direction. She writes very little about these two events, but it is clear that they shifted her towards her conversion, even as she continued her scholarly work and her talks about women in the modern world. Despite her mother's grief and near disowning of her, she entered a Carmelite convent, where she wrote her two major books, one called *Finite and Eternal Being* and the other a study of Saint John of the Cross, *The Science of the Cross*, which was never completed. From the moment she entered the convent, she told everyone she knew not to vote for Hitler at any cost, never hiding or denying her Jewish background but reiterating her belief that her conversion was an inevitable extension of it.

At 5 P.M. on August 2, 1942, she was assembled in the choir with the other nuns and was reading aloud the writing that they would meditate upon the next day when two SS men came in looking for her. They said, "In ten minutes she has to leave the house." She prayed with the sisters and packed a blanket, a cup, a spoon, and food for three days; this was all the SS men said they thought she would need. Edith asked the nuns, "Pray for me and notify the Swiss consul." At this time Westerbork, a transit station, was holding 1,200 Catholic Jews, and Edith Stein became known in those few days as exceptionally generous. She wrote to her prioress from there saying "I am happy with everything" and she also asked for warm clothes and blankets for her sister Rosa, who was with her. Also with her were six other nuns and three Trappist brothers of Jewish descent. Already all of them had been forced to wear a Jewish star and had a red *J* stamped on their identity cards. As this group was transported by train from Holland to Auschwitz, Stein managed to leave three notes behind:

one with a stationmaster, one with a former pupil of hers who was standing on a platform, and one with a stranger saying "We are traveling east." Her prison number was 44074. She was killed on the vigil of St. Laurence, August 9. (W. H. Auden wrote: "In Hell, as in prison and the army, its inhabitants are identified not by name but by number. They do not have numbers, they are numbers.")

The continuing quarrel over the political value of her murder— was she one Jew among millions or was she a Christian martyr?— would probably strike her as deeply ironic, given her stated conviction that Jews and Christians had an unbreakable bond, one that might as well be called "family." She did not expect to die so she can hardly be called a martyr, but she was not just pretending to be a Carmelite nun at the time of being chosen to die—as a Jew. That she selected the most extreme way of expressing her Catholicism—by living it out in a convent—can't be separated from her commitment to her own thought. A reconstruction of her life that would ignore what she herself said about it is the ultimate erasure.

Stein wrote that the possibility of scholarship's being a religious activity only dawned on her while studying Thomas Aquinas. In the years before her conversion she would define herself as a phenomenologist, and she continued throughout her life to define herself this way in relation to her working method. What does that mean?

In the phenomenological system, it is the opposition between worldly and extraworldly (between being and meaning) that is the heart of the human predicament. On the side of the worldly stands the psychological and perceptual subject. On the side of the extra-worldly is the transcendental ego, the *I* who knows. It is this *I* who gives meaning to the psychological subject. Aquinas had described in depth what it means to be a person. In the phenomenological model, a potentially irreconcilable antagonism lies between the transcendent and the physical subject as the source of existential anxiety, while in the Thomist model there is no division between source, consciousness, and person. The mind is an organ of the soul and the spirit is indivisible from the flesh.

From the Ganges to Lake Anza there is a divine spirit that allows no vacuum. *"Anima forma corporis,"* wrote Aquinas; the soul gives the body its form so that a person evolves in relation to a doubling experience—from the spirit (God) within to the spirit (God) outside the flesh. The human as "the image of God" is only such to the extent that the human exists in that reflective position relative to the creator. A person offends God when she does something that is not for her own good because union with God (reunion with the good) is the one desire that is common to all.

The way that circumstances unfold and confront a person, and the way that reason and consciousness have to contend with each other in response to arriving circumstances, is what makes phenomenology seem familiar to anyone reading Aquinas. The difference, however, is the difference between up and down, first and last, beginning and end. To Aquinas the whole structure derives its form from an unknowable and invisible source that we can interpret through our own behaviors.

In her work on empathy while still a student in Freiburg, Stein made her first serious contribution to philosophy. She wrote of her work on this essay, "Each morning I seated myself at my desk with some trepidation. I was like a tiny dot in limitless space. Would anything come to me out of this great expanse—anything that I could grasp? I lay back as far as I could in my chair and strenuously focused my mind on what at the moment I deemed the most vital question. After a while, it seemed as though light began to dawn. Then I was able, at least, to formulate a question and to find ways to attack it. And as soon as one point became clear, new questions arose in various directions."

Her paper "On the Problem of Empathy" was, in terms of its style, nothing like the above account of writing it. In fact the academic style she adopted was almost unreadable—it lacked the fluidity of experience or any way of speaking directly, and rested instead on a carefully constructed logic as stiff as wood. For instance in one passage of this paper she wrote, "There is given together with the apprehended material in a co-givenness, all that which does not fall into the senses at the time but which might do so. . . . And the apprehension of which might be achieved during the progress of the perceptions." The perplexing difference in style between her recollection of how the work came to be written and the written work itself becomes for me the subject of that work. She writes as if she is in exile from the landscape of the language confronting her.

While her account of herself writing shows a pleasurable awareness of all that does *not* fall within the range of her control, her writing on empathy is just the opposite: highly controlled, dedicated to defending a sequence of logical propositions that don't seem to be her own. There is no sense of air and arrival. Is this just because the first person—her "I"—has been banished from the essay as being an inappropriate guest at the table of ideas? Closing the grammatical system off from the presence of the writer is often a way of banishing bewilderment from the prose. The "I" is the wild card that someone with her training does not allow in the deck. It undetermines the overdetermined. To be a questing presence in her own written sentence would be a symptom of uncertainty and would thereby undermine the whole system she was defending.

Later Stein as an advocate for women—shortly after her conversion and before her entrance into the Carmelite convent in Cologne—describes a good person as expansive, quiet, empty of self, warm, and clear. Here her prose style contains exactly those qualities, and in her essays on women's issues, especially education, she writes in relaxed and accessible sentences, reiterating her themes in ways that make her both present and objective. A woman who attended one of her lectures wrote, "Edith Stein's lecture was the most convincing because it was free of the pathos of the feminist movement and because the speaker herself markedly and visibly personified her own thoughts."

In those years her engagement in women's issues, which accompanied her rejections by the patriarchal academies, warms up her language. Her uncompleted autobiography, *Life in a Jewish Family (1891–1916)*, describes her home and school life until her graduation from Freiburg with a degree of Doctor of Philosophy, an achievement which would get her almost nowhere in terms of an academic career. In this book of recollections, her style, as it is in her letters, is serious in its effort to describe things well, but it is also full of humor, opinion, and affection. Written after her work on empathy and during the progress of her immersion in theology, her writing style in this autobiography is almost novelistic in its attention to character and cultural detail. This book, written for the German public as an introduction to the quality of life in an ordinary Jewish family, is neither apologetic nor intimate. Its tone is softer and more subtle than in any of her other formal work, however, indicating a shift in compositional method.

How does a change in vocabulary save your life? Replacing one word with another word for the same thought—can this actually transform your feelings about things? Even after she stopped writing academic papers on phenomenology, Stein continued to talk about the emptiness surrounding both objects and perceptions as being part of our experience of them. She suggested that emptiness—space—teaches us to mistrust the location of the "I" inside us, since it exists at a "zero point of orientation," being both at the source of the physical body and on its periphery where it, too, becomes empty. Space subsumes the structure of the person by waiting for it. Empty space precedes, succeeds, and accompanies our motions. But if all it is doing is absorbing and dissolving us in our approach, then we are beyond poverty of spirit. We live in dread because our body is unrecognizable in relation to a void that swallows the last location of the ego. The person actually knows the planet and the cosmos better than she knows her own self that disappears. She is unfamiliar to her own self. The Zohar—a collection of mystical interpretations of the Pentateuch—talks abut this phenomenon, occurring when "the supreme Point and the World-to-come ascend" and where the end and the beginning become inseparable. The Zohar, however, calls this point Zero, the Supreme Will, or God.

Stein begins to feel that this emptiness (Zero) contains something that wants to be found in the way it surrounds a person, waits for it and seems to continue personal consciousness; it precedes one's perception of being in one place. Now she calls the body "the illuminated surface." And she wonders if anything *not* known can exist as an image in the human mind. Is it possible to imagine another world ("God"?) or are we condemned to a knowing that is based in our limited perceptions?

Hope is an "intuition of emptiness" with which we make an agreement each time we take a step. Each time we exert our will we are exhibiting hope inside emptiness. And over time all the necessary actions that we take will help us develop a familiarity with objects and with space that makes our comforts seem natural rather than adopted. We begin to trust the logic of our own and the world's machinery working in tandem and forget the mysterious disjunctures between hopes and arrivals. Yet the emptiness remains always in place, an experience that is part of each place. This emptiness she begins to call "God" and the location of this emptiness both outside and within us in relation to those things and people who exist alongside us is also "God." (Husserl himself wrote, "I have attempted to open a way to God, without God, so that men may find their way back to God.")

Writing the name "God" poses a problem since an image of God, as one knows and understands God, can only be empty, negative, *not* sayable. Indeed rituals and devotional objects serve the purpose of reminding us that named things are *not* God. When people kneel in front of figures and kiss the stone feet of Christ, they are kneeling and kissing the facts that are *not* God but are intended to remind us of God by this specifically-addressed *not*ness. (As the priest and philosopher Pavel Florensky said about the ikon, "[I]t is the outline of a vision . . . nothing but a board!") The word "God" stills the language around it because it is a name that refers to nothing knowable by our perceptions.

The Zohar says that the Divine Presence "cannot be known, nor how it makes beginning or end, just as the zero number produces beginning and end." The guiding instruction here is that any way we look we encounter zero ("God") and anywhere zero rests, it encounters no one. In a word, there is either an echo of an infused first-meaning or there is terror. If God allows God to be found in each experience, it will be more than part of each experience. Its essence will precede the existence of the experience and form it into a corresponding essence.

In 1930 Stein wrote to a friend who was a nun, "After every encounter in which I am made aware how powerless we are to exercise direct influence, I have a deeper sense of the urgency of my own *holocaustum.*" That is, renunciation, sacrifice. . . . Her failure to get the work that she was trained for, her disappointment in love, and undoubtedly more setbacks than these contributed to her withdrawal from the world, as they do with so many of us. The older people are at the time of their conversion, the more likely it is that their defenses to the given world have broken down and the old words are worn out. But the fact that she thought of herself as a living sacrifice to unpredictability and injustice is what marks her conversion in particular. She seems to have had an insight into the nature of sacrifice as a world-act, much as Tarkovsky in his film *The Sacrifice* did. She was fully aware by then of the gluttonous inner belly of the Third Reich. If a person makes the decision to be the thing that history and chance are already making them be, this decision switches the mechanisms away from the fated into a zone of freedom. This is one definition of a religious act, as it is also of a selfless political act.

While she continued to develop her theories on women, Catholic pedagogy, Thomism, and phenomenology, she began a close reading and study of Saint John of the Cross, the father of the Carmelite Reform and friend of Saint Teresa. Her attraction to him must have been deeply empathic; he had a developed theology of negativity; he had lived through difficult times; and he was a poet. Writing about him, her syntax remained dull as if under the corrective eye of Husserl. But it still gives the impression that she is learning something from Saint John that she avidly wants to understand. Maybe she is learning how to write poetry; his inspired language must have seemed a complete mystery, the diametric opposite of her own.

He was the kind of poet who wrote with full consciousness of his purpose. His syntax, the unifying sounds of his poems from the first line to the last, indicated that he was the same person at the beginning that he was at the end. He was not writing to find out what he knew and through writing become someone new. He wrote the poems, and wrote about them as one who already knew, before he wrote, what he was going to discover and what each word intended for him. The resolution of the whole poem was there from the start, the way Dante glimpsed Paradise before he began his descent into hell.

You can live through anything if you know that all will be well in the end.

+ + +

He compared the cross to the image of the tree in Paradise, now with its fruit all eaten, a wooden stake on which God has been slain. He believed that it is best to make nothingness your goal, if only in order to preserve the freedom of the spirit that is at the heart of all things. The Doctor of Nada, he was called. (In his later life Saint John liked to carve crosses from wood and give them away. Sometimes he kneeled on broken earthenware, and sometimes he cut his feet on bare rocks but didn't seem to feel the pain. He kneeled between the bed and the wall to say his rosary in a small room full of skulls and crosses. "On that wood we murder what is good" is what he said. He was so intensely feminine one could imagine his breasts—like those of Saint Francis—producing milk, and he described as "the shy and fleeting glance of the hart on the hill" the way that Christ appears to a person.)

In Stein's book on Saint John she developed her theology of suffering, using the cross (not a sharp enough symbol for the world we live in now) as her central symbol. (The cross—after the exterminations/holocausts of the twentieth century—seems more problematic than anything. It seems to represent the limit of human imagination: either a locked gate where humans end up staring in horror at what they have done and are doomed to repeat, or a weapon used to torch others.) What can a wooden stake burning with such messages teach us today that is redemptive? Stein saw the cross as the body itself, a stick figure, so to speak, of the human form. The bones ached and the heart was broken. The interior body-cross was substance that suffered. In this vision a life was acted out on the cross of its own body from the moment of birth.

+ + +

Stein's brothers and sisters began fleeing Germany for America. For a reader of her life this exodus signals her own fate in Auschwitz. Like everyone in the world she could not foresee her end; but the reader can, and is given the unusual opportunity to know and to discover at the same time. You watch the shadow grow longer and thicker while she grows happier and more full of belief. She begins to write poetry for occasions in her convent and for her own pleasure. *The Science of the Cross* was the last book she wrote.

She wrote to a friend: "What is our life like? Early in the morning, just about three hours in the choir; one hour of meditation, the Little Hours, Mass. Then about two hours of work. This working time is filled differently by each one, but it has to be used well by all of us. For several years I was allowed to use it mostly for intellectual work."

"He whom we must love is absent," wrote Simone Weil. One could suggest that "he whom we love must be absent" from the lives of certain women with metaphysical goals for themselves. If—as some say—Edith Stein had loved someone, a Catholic, say, a student (Hans Lipps) who was at the university with her in Freiburg, and if her family talked her out of marrying him because of his religion, it would not be strange if she now had an extra-emotional motive for conversion. Assuming the religious (or political) identity of an absent but once-beloved person is not an uncommon choice. The story of Ruth has resonated for as long as it has because of its psychological truth. Traditions are transformed, broken, and erased in women's bodies; and in the secret imaginative lives of both men and women unbreakable marriages take place.

(Weil also wrote that "there is an unspeakable wrench in the soul at the separation of a desire from its object.")

It seems that a voluntary celibate makes her body into the place where nothing but light is falling and cells are breathing. Her senses experience emptiness and silence as indicators of what is *not* present in the sense of *too* present. To the voluntary celibate emptiness and silence are welcome, they travel alongside and await you. Unlike things that you put on for a short time, then leave "behind" in time and place—things that acquire histories based in their tragically illuminated surfaces—emptiness and silence are liberations from saddening matter. In Carmel they acquire a shape and presence that form a reverse prototype of marriage; in Carmel one is wedded to Christ. While there are no loving looks or touches in this situation, there is apparently a freedom and a transparency to being alone. The body becomes an easy channel for the invisible. You may be lonely but are not empty.

One could say that the concealment of certain women in history has been a willed action. In other words, rather than reading silence as repression, you can read it as a means of liberation. Stein herself wrote that "for the accomplishment of great things for the Church, the Lord preferred to choose women who forgot themselves completely: for example, St. Brigid, St. Catherine of Siena, and St. Teresa, the mighty reformer at the time of the great apostasy." Stein's convent experience followed many years of speaking on behalf of women and expanding the concept of motherliness to a near-ideology.

The rapture that lights up Saint John's poetry also runs

through the writings of Ganges poets and philosophers (Sankara, Ramanuja, Ramakrishna, Ramana Maharishi, Yogananda, etc.) and other mystics. It is a rapture that seeps out of reversals of conventional relationships. In John's Trinity "the Holy Spirit is the burn, the hand is the Father, and the touch is the Son."

A turning inside out of physical perception is the hope behind voluntary celibacy. What we think of as being a metaphor—a correspondence between the images of the world and the feelings they inspire in us—seems to be reversed for the long-term solitary. Unlike the body of a beloved lover whose arms and legs enfold you, give you joy, then part and depart, the air and your own senses of hearing, seeing, feeling become your companions and spiritual oxygen. They stay with you. The visible world is soon emblematic of the intentions of the invisible. Invisible, as in Amor, comes first. . . . And then there are buildings, walls, streets on which you find yourself walking, objects that rise out of a timeless ahead and seem to have been waiting for you.

Where else, according to John, but in the senses ("the illuminated surface") is the mystic supposed to experience rapture? Saint Teresa felt her ecstasy in her groin and Saint Therese of Lisieux, dying, did and wrote poetry about it. The location of the sensation doesn't contaminate the disposal of the spirit. The Carmelites, who have housed several spectacular poets and mystics, are committed celibates married to Christ. They have a ceremony with bridal dresses and rings. They encourage a relationship between the body's parts and its perceptions that is the reverse of the usual order. One is not so much running from object to object as receiving the future, which is empty. The wedding dress marks the start of a period of waiting. William

Blake, a solitary who was not celibate, saw himself coming to meet himself.

"You leave in the soul an affect and a feeling that are so beneficent that every touch of creatures seems gross and deceitful to it," writes John to God. The soul is his word for this interior organ of perception that hides behind the seen skin. It has a shape, it is the potential *purusa* in Hinduism, the transformed one, Jesus after the Resurrection. "For God normally grants no favor to the body that he has not first and principally bestowed on the soul . . . so all the more intense is the external pain in the wound of the body. And one grows together with the other." For John, as for many Ganges mystics and philosophers, the interior, invisible body determines the form and substance of the material body.

Stein began writing poetry for occasions in her convent and for herself. Some of that poetry is sad and thick and thoughtful— weighed down by memory, or by her identification with victims of Germany's war:

1939 POEM

Bless those who are tormented
and the loneliness that is an abyss, and bless
the uneasiness of human beings
and the sorrow that can never be expressed.

Bless the moths moving at night
through unknown forms and shadows
and bless the distress of people dying now
and grant them peace in their souls.

Bless those whose hearts are clouded
and to the sick bring relief, and above all peace

to the tortured. Teach those at a friend's grave
to forget, and free those who feel guilty, free them all.

Bless the happy, Lord, and protect their happiness.
I am in mourning and my shoulders are heavy
from the weight of this cloth, but give me strength
and I will keep going, as a penitent, to my grave.

Then bless my sleep among all the departed.
Remember that your son suffered agony for us
and in the mercy you provide for all human needs
include eternal peace in the grave.

This poem goes to the root of her personality—her maternalism, her distance from others, her relationship to God which is personal and hopeful, her guilt, her feeling of being clothed in emotions, her interest in both justice and mercy, her obedience to certain conventions, her disappointment.

Disappointment is an insidious killer. It brings you down with small, repeated blows. Stein had suffered it deeply on numerous occasions and in many forms. ("I have not the heart to ask X to use his influence on my behalf since philosophy in Hamburg is already represented by two Jewish professors.") The arrival of the SS was obviously the ultimate disappointment and one can only read backwards from there. The Pope didn't save her, neither did her convent, neither did poetry or any other interest or alliance. To call her a martyr is somehow to suggest that she chose that hour and that way. Saint John was also dragged off to prison where he didn't want to be. His uncovering in that darkness the secret to his theology is lucky for us, but it's not for us to say that it was lucky for him too. That he didn't die there was lucky for him.

The Divine for Stein, as it was for Saint John, was black—an "All-penetrating ray" of blackness, "merciful, yet unrelenting," which "fills the soul with fear at the sight of her own existence." Her work with John's poetry may well have been among the last experiences she had.

On the subject of what she called "expired experience," this is what she once wrote to a friend, and it sounds like a developed poetics: "Whatever is actual—the Now phase—is always something momentary, and as such has no chance for existence; rather it must become embedded in an experience that in its totality will have some duration. That from which this reality has sprung is—insofar as it no longer belongs to the Now—expired. However, insofar as it necessarily belongs to the unity of the experience and makes possible the ever present Now, it is still alive, not extinguished."

Her close reading of John's poetry may have allowed Stein to develop a new vocabulary and a new syntax. While her concepts are much like the ones she developed beside Husserl, the medium of poetry turns it around:

Who are you, shining in my dark heart?

You draw me along the way a mother's hand once did
and if you let go I couldn't go another inch.
You are the space both surrounding and holding my being
and without you I would vanish into air
out of which you formed me—you who are nearer to me
than I am to my own self, more interior but nowhere.

This is how you smash through every word and name—

Holy spirit—
Eternal love!

In this poem she continues to explore her obsession with the presence of a void that never-endingly offers both static and moving objects up to the person. But her naming of that void ("mother," "love") is a triumph over her earlier rhetoric of despair. She has literally used words as functions of self-salvation.

The poetics of Saint John's theology is built *in* blackness and built *of* blackness; his night realism is that emptiness where naming ends. Its tradition is apophatic. Dionysius the Areopagite spilled his theology from a ray of darkness and out came the material. In the Upanishads, one prayer says, "May he who is one without color, who by the exercise of his power in his hidden purpose breathes forth this many-colored creation and finally gathers it into himself, give us the grace of a clear vision." Blackness is the source of all color, form, substance in this tradition.

In May of 1941 Stein was working on an essay about the symbolic theology of the Areopagite, "Ways To Know God: The 'Symbolic Theology' of Dionysius the Areopagite and Its Factual Presuppositions." It was published posthumously. She wrote a friend in language very different from that in the title of the essay, "The ray of illumination that (according to Dionysius) descends on us after having passed through all nine Choirs (of angels) connects the entire grace-inundated spirit world; the Trinity is personally present on every level; even in the lowest choir of angels it is he himself whom we meet. It is not his unapproachable majesty that God communicates to us through his messengers but rather his overflowing love. It is their bliss, just as it will be ours (and already is to some extent), to be allowed to cooperate in God's dispensing of graces."

At what point, this kind of writing makes me ask, does the renaming of things actually transform the world around you? Can it? Can you build a vocabulary of faith out of a rhetoric first made of dread and then stand behind this new language? Is faith created by a shift in rhetoric, one that can be consciously constructed, or must there be a shattering experience, one that trashes the old words for things? The difference between her two rhetorics—one hardcore philosophy, one dogmatic-spiritual—makes one wonder how they can coexist, when each one is (seemingly) unbelievable in relation to the other. Only in some of her poems (and her life) do they become indivisible.

With the other Carmelite sisters she chose to be immured and liberated simultaneously. Walls in this case served as guards facing outwards, just as the Immaculate Conception of Mary can be interpreted as an idea (sustained by women) that tries to break with the repeated violence in women's lives rather than as an idea that seeks to idealize virginity. Stein's withdrawal into a convent represented a radical and daring reversal of all her training as a scholar and activist; it turned her commitment to reevaluating women in society into a life among women outside society. It was a real effort at revolution—more than conversion, it was an effort at creating a new person.

The bridal ceremony, peculiar to Carmelites, was the outer sign of her internal transformation from a philosopher into a religious. About this ceremony she wrote, "In the bridal union God surrounds the soul with a love that cannot be compared even with the tenderest love of a mother. He gives it His breast, he reveals his secrets to it." She who had started out as a skeptical thinker and remained one who used the phenomenological method became a poet who was married to a spirit. The silk white wedding dress she wore at her ceremony in April 1934 at the Carmel of Cologne-Lindenthal was afterwards made into a chasuble. In 1944 the convent was destroyed during a bombing attack, but this vestment was saved and continued to have a history of its own.

WHITE LINES

Ilona Karmel, born in Cracow in 1925, was sixteen when she was deported to a German labor camp for the duration of the war.

Later, seriously and permanently injured by German tanks during the liberation of Buchenwald, she made her way to the U.S. where she studied, taught, and wrote two novels in English. Both could be called prison novels although one was set in a postwar hospital.

In both *Stephania* and *An Estate of Memory* Karmel walks doubt into a furnace of gestural and physical details and leaves it there.

The question "What is one person's responsibility for another?" moves into a farther, more chthonic place of uncertainty than most people ever have to go.

As Karmel herself remarked, her books attempt to speak about historic destruction and the human search for hope, not just survival. In *An Estate of Memory* "each of the characters, though inmate of a concentration camp, is an 'Everywoman' deprived of the automatic nobility which those who equate commemoration with adulation tend to bestow upon victims of a historical catastrophe. The question I posed to myself at the outset was: would the pressure of an extreme situation leave these characters any room for free choice, any possibility for a gratuitous act? If, at the end, the characters choose a sacrificial death, it is I hope not because of an *a priori* scheme, but because the trials and errors of their inner growth make this choice inescapable."

Her characters struggle with the confines of their circumstances, mostly women trying to cooperate and cohabit, and don't wait for God to intervene or anyone else. Their memories— unhappy and happy—may be all that they have.

And in this sense they, more than most others, have got a stake in subjectivity.

A prisoner or a patient becomes a double monster—despised and then despising of self and others, unless she can redraw the content of the experience, and give it a new name.

The prisoner of a jail or hospital has to enter into a radical self-examination or be at the mercy of clocks and routines. Meister Eckhart in a sermon says: "Being attached to work that does not bring you face to face with God and the freedom God offers is like 'a year.' It is not a now, but a year to be so enslaved."

A person is often forced to seek salvation through subjectivity in the most meaningless times in order to endure those times.

Karmel once remarked that the Holocaust brought God back to the Jews, who had been thoroughly secularized in the years leading up to the Third Reich.

She had no tolerance for the aestheticization of suffering. She didn't place the Holocaust above the cruelties enacted in Russia, Cambodia, Palestine, or Africa, the local hospital or prison. Her single interest was ontological and she came to the conclusion that "what we sense and hope for is rooted in what we inescapably are."

A prison is as good a place as any to find this out, because any prison is a laboratory in which a human life is tested for the survival of itself, its humanness.

Prison days unfold according to random (unjust) rules and punishments.

The prison system manipulates the people it incarcerates in order to see if they can be deformed and become something unrecognizable. "What are they if they are like me?" a warden might wonder.

There is no higher logic behind the logic of punishment.

The slippery body of its endless amendments and its casual outcomes is the one on which people commit suicide or find an alternative freedom.

"Before our eyes hath the substance been plundered; torn and stripped from us."

The prisoner, when deformed, is required to endure the gift of self-loathing. When a prisoner, contrarily, finds something recognizable in herself, then she can be at least mentally liberated. Remembrance is one approach to self-recognition and reorganizing the facts through writing them down as transformed moments is another.

+ + +

"Behind the highway the houses stood, big, heavy quadrangles, darker than the air of the night, their massive bodies punctuated by the brightly lit windows. They looked like blocks of dominoes, black with the light points engraved in them. But farther away the houses merged into one with the sky and the night, and the glittering windows seemed to be incrusted in the dark air." (*An Estate of Memory*)

The importance of Karmel's novel—its bitter inheritance of memory—lies in its depiction of the camp as the condition of the Western world in mid-century. The labor camp is not an aberration but a continuation of humanity's increasing contempt for itself. Weary history is a one-way street with no U-turns, no exits.

Progress creates its own problems like an artist who creates the problem he then sets out to study. The concentration camp experiments with the outcome of the way things are already headed. It asks, What if? and tries it.

Therefore, both of Karmel's novels are almost unbearably hard to read, relentless in their cataloguing of daily events in the depersonalized, oppressed environment. No conspiracy is necessary if one looks hard enough at the slow erosion of a worldview that at least tried to guarantee some obligations between people and their city. The novels exist in isolation—not as "holocaust literature." Their underlying purpose is to face the results of twentieth-century deracination, to salvage one point of reference for persons in our time to live by.

At the service for the eve of Yom Kippur the congregation will say, "We have trespassed, we have dealt treacherously, we have stolen, we have spoken slander, we have committed iniquity, and have done wickedly, we have acted presumptuously, we have committed violence, we have framed falsehood, we have counseled evil . . ." and on into a long litany of failures that paradoxically affirms the existence of a recognizable person.

"If evil is a mystery, then the abyss must remain a mystery that we know only through the glass and darkly, through our sense of deprivation and longing. And through our shabby, always perverted human love," Karmel wrote.

If the inexplicable is named and explained, it enters the world of the justifiable and becomes dangerous. The Chassidim have said, "The greatest sin is when a man forgets he is the son of a King." What this means to Karmel is that self-loathing makes a person demean his anguish and sense of futility; it makes him reduce these to maladjustments that can be cured, accidents of biology.

Karmel found in the Catholic theologian Karl Rahner thoughts which she had had premonitions of, herself, over her lifetime. Mainly these thoughts involve the unthematic, those areas of experience that exist outside of language. She came to believe that writing itself, when it is on track, circles around the unthematic, "shunning too great a familiarity—lest such familiarity violate it."

The name of God has perhaps never been more of a secret than it is now. We all know that the future likes stealth, abjection, secrecy, and smallness. And the future is where God comes in, if one is looking. So in some way the future and God invite thoughts of collapse, the end of the self. The end of words. The future has the look of a nameless expanse. The past is either trapped in the individuated body like water in a rag, or else both past and present are acts of shucking, removing, discarding the gravity of the world's givens as one enters a freer, lighter economy of space. One could think of the material world as something like an air that one runs through at high speed, in order to get past it. This thought would reverse the usual sense of being as being stuck in a body moving along with time.

Just as music leaves itself behind, and words have to be spoken in order to effect their disappearance, one can catch a glimmer of a life itself being a glad renunciation of itself.

The Catholic Church once demonstrated the belief that the brain is the site of consciousness; that the body is not an illusion; that a person can be injured by thoughts. In accepting this situation, the Church tried to influence people, to turn ugly words into radiant ones, to feed each mind with sublime vocabularies. To offer repetition, rhythm, an end to the separation between speaking and hearing.

At least that was her action in past centuries.

But what will happen to language now that the word "God" has fizzled into the existential absurd, so that past and present are buried in instant parries and thrusts from the emptiness ahead?

Literacy and the reading of scripture (in most cultures) were at one time indistinguishable projects. If there is no sacred text can language still be trusted to have an original gust of justice forming it, a virtuous grammar embedded in it, better meanings hidden in the white lines?

Theology is a science without instruments. Only words. Therefore words present its greatest dangers.

No telescopes, no tables, no beakers or microscopes. Its vocabulary is its everything. What is a science? A discipline, a study, a method, knowledge gained by experience. Theology inquires into the nature of God; that's its sole business, while science seeks to uncover the intersections between world and mind, time and space, gone and gene.

But often theology assumes the language of conviction, overdetermining the answers to its own questions. Theology can offer no evidence or proof to show for its conclusions, beyond the magnificence of language. While it is not free from current anxiety about the place of the human in the universe, about the human's right to exist at all, theology is stuck with the word "God" as the beginning of itself and therefore its end.

Strangely, suffering, which is the opposite of "God," is often sentimentalized and even idolized by religious literature.

A contemporary theologian, Johann Metz, has noted, "Is it really only by chance that theology is talking, in an almost euphoric way, about a God who suffers and shares suffering, precisely at a time when aesthetics and aestheticization have taken on a key role in our postmodern sort of worldview? Putting the question differently . . . does not all this talk of the suffering God reveal something like an aestheticization of all suffering?"

+ + +

And later he answers, "Suffering is nothing great and exalted."

And Metz, a liberation theologian, concludes that the idealization of suffering cannot be a good thing, because true suffering is "a frightening symptom that one is no longer able to love."

For many people, their anguish about suffering comes in the form of unarticulated questions directed to the problem of God.

"If there is no God to know what has happened to me, what does any of it mean or matter? If the injustices I have suffered are not accounted for in the mind of God, then how can I live with them? How can words, pouring and sorting according to rhetorical formulas, give a true account of the difficulty of my days? Why live through these humiliations unless there is some record? Some justice? Some evidence?"

This idea of a Zeus-like Judge may only impede the questioner's chances of a liberating revelation about suffering.

Even the word "father" may be fatally tainted by history.

Both words, when saturated with expectations of love returned and mercy exacted, fail in the world after all. It takes a massive delusional move to think that injustice and cruelty are promulgated by a fatherly God for a reason from which we are excluded, unless that God is truly sadistic.

For as soon as God is given attributes like good, loving, all-powerful, God necessarily becomes a collaborator with evil.

In some ways atheism offers better insurance for the Void named God—to exist as pure unknown—than religion. Even the word

Universe may be cleaner than God, and DNA better than Father. Certainly more and more people find the idea of Karma— another version of DNA—easier to understand than the Trinity.

But while atheism might be the best protection for God, it was the power of atheism in the twentieth century that enflamed the huge and vicious massacres, organized around technology and torture, culture and territory.

The loss of confidence in that single word, God, has thrown other words into a crisis. Like a fragmented and random reading of the night sky, language floats out of throats and brains helter skelter. "One finally experiences oneself as a kind of newspaper— so many headings, so many items jumbled together with no connection that bears witness to our transcendental part. So does guilt, so does the longing for the unmercenary act, so does the rebellion against being partially described—be it by a science or by another person—arise."

It is possible that we have almost everything backwards. Like the pilot who avoids a plane crash by reading a computer instead of looking out the window or calling the person below in charge, the human readings are at a second or third remove from the actual. The sacrifice here is the pilot—the person—himself. His own perceptions are useless. He has become an instrument of an instrument. He and the thing function in tandem as two things.

It is perhaps lucky that the spoken word remains wild inside of us, rushing and vanishing out of our bodies.

Speech is not thought, often not even "of thought." Speech is a form of breath. It emerges as units of meaning, letters, words, sentences that are forgotten before they are remembered and are uttered in a near state of oblivion. The hearer hears what the speaker forgets in the act of speaking. And what the speaker intends emerges backwards in the speaker's consciousness. The units of sound last only as long as the breath is able. The heart supplants the head.

"What matters lives, hidden or not, within us so that when the right words come we recognize them as something we tried to say but did not know how."

Listening is existing in the future of all utterance.

So the future is full of listening, wanting, and understanding.

But what a speaker intends to say is rarely fulfilled in the sentence; and if its intention is over-intended, it loses its capacity for arousing attention in the hearer.

Part of the force of speech comes with its emotional risk. One hears units and tones more than particular words or facts and attends to these. It is possible that people want to hear poetry, whether they like it or not. Their brains and ears want it.

"One is seized," Aquinas said about the experience of being "found" by God.

"Being a phenomenon of language, the poem can be in its essence dialogical, a message sent out in a bottle—certainly in the not-always hopeful belief that somewhere sometime it will be washed onto land, into heartland perhaps. This is how poems travel: oriented towards something; towards something that stands open, that can be occupied, perhaps towards a Thou that can be spoken to, a reality that can be addressed. A poem, I think, is about such realities."

Ilona Karmel referred to these lines of Paul Celan's as her *Flaschenpost*. He wrote them after reading a poem by the Russian poet Ye. A. Boratynksky:

> My talent is small and I am not famous
> But I live—and there is someone
> To whom my existence is dear.
> The distant one, he who comes after me
> Will find in my verse my soul.
> Who can tell? My soul might connect with him
> And just as I found a friend in my generation
> So will I find a reader in the future.

The sending out of words to a blind future is what any writer does. It is a simple occupation (nothing special, chosen, or justifiable) that replicates the sending of messages without envelopes, speech traveling forward to a listener. It reproduces the sensation of being all mechanics and body, loaded with events, and projected onto a blind No One. It echoes the turning around of Orpheus in the underworld, because he wouldn't have been a poet if he hadn't turned. Why should he have trusted anything but his instincts? Everything is there while everything is Orpheus.

> Save it,
> before
> the Stone Day has blown dry
>
> the swarms of men

and beasts, just
as the seven-reed flute mandates,
in front of mouth and muzzle.
— *Paul Celan*

Ilona Karmel read poetry passionately when she was dying and in the hospital. She blamed her pride for the fact that she had not done so earlier. Certain poems struck her as wonderfully unthematic. "Is that why you prefer poetry to prose? Is that why you insist on the opaqueness of true poetry?" she asked.

(Almost all the quoted prose passages in this piece come from a handwritten letter I received from Ilona Karmel in 1998 and didn't read closely until after she had died. It followed on discussions we had had over the preceding years.)

"There is a Chassidic story saying: Why was the miracle Elijah the Prophet performs so great (when he caused the idols to be consumed by fire)? No one said how great is Elijah. Everyone said how great is God—that is why it is a true miracle."

THE CONTEMPORARY LOGOS

1. Adam and Eve heard the First One's voice "in the garden walking" with them. This voice—Memra in Hebrew—was Yahweh, the Law, the Logos, and it was moving around beside them like a radio with legs. This same voice of the Logos was later heard speaking to Moses, whose face, afterwards, burned like hot gold until no one dared go near him.

2. The sound of that voice comes and goes in other human and angelic forms throughout Scripture; then it recedes and disappears. The Gnostics felt it fading into eternity and becoming that eternity. The Logos spread out so far, and became so thin after the crucifixion, that contact with it from them on occurred only in much the same way as Proust's involuntary memory experience: "It depends on chance whether we come upon it before we die or whether we never encounter it."

3. To the Gnostic, this sensational moment of encounter with Truth was only given to a soul by chance. It was eternity granting temporality a fleeting reprieve. Otherwise, the best that the mind could do for a person was to channel an original voice from and into the empty heavens.

4. The gospel according to Marcion was a radical response to the Yahweh of the Torah. He, as an early Gnostic Christian, believed that this old Yahweh represented the world and temporality and was, therefore, a false representation of the actual disappeared God. For Marcion, the serpent in the Garden of Eden was, in fact, the true god—the one who is forever alien on this earth. Alien: separate, other, outside, unassimilable.

5. This, Marcion's theory, was blasted by Philo the Alexandrian, who was a Platonist. For Philo, Yahweh in the Torah showed us the commandments central to thought and language: prudence, temperance, courage. Philo believed that the Logos (our source) showed us the way to understand ourselves and our actions. That is, Scripture. He believed that nothing written in Scripture was empty of meaning. Each phrase had a hidden, revelatory message.

6. "And you shall put manifestation and truth in the oracle of judgment." Philo took this line from Exodus and interpreted in this way: "The oracle here meant the organs of speech which exist in us, the power of language . . . and in this beloved kind of language there are two supreme virtues—namely, distinctiveness and truth." Philo believed that the human mouth could operate

as a kind of oracle only if the person was speaking justly. The Logos then would be entering the world through words saturated in the body of a human being. It would be revealed in its ideal state and through a mouth.

7. Marcion, who didn't believe in a continuing connection between the creator and the created, read the story of Jesus as proof of his position. Marcion believed that Jesus came into the world to show how humanity had been duped by the story of Yahweh, the false and worldly God. The Passion of Jesus made it clear to Marcion that God was distant, alien, indifferent, his back turned. This position had followers and influence. Christian Gnostics agreed with Marcion that the serpent's injunction to "eat of the tree of Knowledge" was the advice of the true alien God who wanted us to know that we are abandoned in nature.

8. Many recent thinkers shared this attitude, including Simone Weil when she wrote, "We must take the feeling of being at home into exile. We must be rooted in the absence of a place." (She herself suffered terribly from homesickness.)

9. The Zohar: "The finite word of man was aimed at the infinite word of God."

10. Beckett's characters speak for, in, and out of an awareness of infinity as the cause of an alienation so complete it is absurd to make a home in it. The strangeness in his writing begins in an uncertainty about whether he is writing out of infinity or into it. The mouth as a contemporary oracle floats in a void.

The French poet Edmond Jabès wrote of his writing: "I have entered each book of mine with the very clear impression that I was not expected, or, rather, that I had been expected so long they finally despaired of my coming."

"They" are his words, or characters, and the sentiment here is the complete opposite of faith. The mind is empty, like the page it approaches, a slate on the lookout for the arrival of words— words that wander in by chance.

But later Jabès wonders, "Is writing simply the way in which that which expressed itself without us nevertheless expresses itself through what has been handed down to us from our origins and which the word has made us discover?"

Do we discover particle theory or does it discover us?
     Do writers really believe what they are writing?
     Or are they airing and testing the language?

11. In *First Love,* by Beckett, there are no illegitimate children, only illegitimate fathers. This problem of origin is not acted out through an empty mouth in this story, but through an ear. "At first I heard nothing, then the voice again, but only just, so faintly did it carry. First I didn't hear it, then I did, I must therefore have begun hearing it, at a certain point, but no, there was no beginning, the sound emerged so softly from the silence and resembled it. . . ."

12. Legitimacy and search—in conversion narratives there is the same need for proof of legitimacy. How does the other person reveal with authority what lies behind his face: an experience so profound it has created a new identity? In torture sessions, too, the other body is squeezed and broken in an effort to release words of value. If that body is a mechanism, the inquisitor's is too. Legitimacy is reduced to a matter of convincing speech.

Doubt has a lot in common with infinity, being boundless, and the authority of what is presented as truthful may be more unsettling than what remains a conjecture. The alien father of the Gnostics, the true God, may have left a little imprint here on earth, but he doesn't seem to care in the way the interfering God of the Torah did. Evil is powerful because it makes itself known very viscerally; it cares, the way the torturer cares. The devil is in the details.

13. The fleeing father in search of his absent father scoots through Beckett's work with the clack of a skeleton running from a cemetery garden. In *First Love*, as the narrator departs from the cries of his own child, he writes, "The cries pursued me down the stairs and out into the street. I stopped before the house door and listened. I could still hear them. If I had not known there was crying in the house I might not have heard them. But knowing it I did. I was not sure where I was. I looked among the stars and constellations for the Wains, but could not find them. And yet they must have been there. My father was the first to show them to me. He had shown me others, but alone, without him beside me, I could never find any but the Wains. . . ."

This ebb and flow of paternity creates the ultimate vertigo. Seed scattered from where? Jesus the Logos says, "When you see a man who was born without a mother, bow down, face to the ground, and adore him. He is your creator." And later he blesses the woman who is barren because, he says, "She knows who her father is." To have no mother and to be a mother to no one is to break with material history. The structural difference between the anonymous ejaculation of the father and the comfortable gestation inside the mother is what has made God into a male. But is the creator ambivalent and uncertain of his own paternal legitimacy?

14. In the Old Testament the voice in the garden, Memra, means the wisdom that flows without ceasing in the human mind. It is inaudible, not even a whisper, and is located in thought which is silent. Sometimes—out of this silence—there is a whisper, and this is when Yahweh manifests that which comes as a parade of thought words with the sound of Itself. It enters thought and speaks softly. In Vedantism a person hears a loud clang between the ears when he or she has crossed over from the material to the unmanifest.

15. When words are mouthed through Beckett's characters—centuries after the crucifixion of Christ—affliction, silence, and history have torn them from an origin. The problem for writers is the same problem for theologians.

+ + +

"This is the point in affliction where we are no longer able to bear either that it should go on or that we should be delivered from it," writes Weil. ("I can't go on, I go on," writes Beckett.)

And then Weil also says, "Nothing that exists is absolutely worthy of love. We must therefore love that which does not exist."

Whether she believed what she wrote is the question that applies to all writing. In her mind the relics of God are to be found in mathematics, music, art, intelligence, poetry, and the eucharist. One can believe in those.

16. What is a contemporaneous moment? It is a now! that unifies disparate pieces of a day, a mind, a history, consciousness, text, etc. It is a kind of intersection. An overlap as in the vulva-shape where two circles intersect with each other. It is a little like the "interlinear" that Walter Benjamin uses to describe a perfect translation. Poetic language combines literalness with an overview of its own construction. There is a fusion of looking and hearing, re-looking and re-hearing.

There is closure even in stream of consciousness, for instance. Only so many words will pour out. Then the mind turns back and inward and begins negating and reconstructing the first thoughts. This is the economy of thinking. When you say "It works now" about a piece of writing, you mean it is finished, closed, and the economy is integrated.

17. I know that a sentence contains only as much language as it can bear, and so it can be viewed as an image of temporality. You cannot turn a *you* into a *she*, a *run* into a *ran*, midsentence, with-

out disrupting the historical accuracy that the sentence is fiercely attempting to protect.

18. Poetry makes severe judgments on itself, writing over itself. It wants to be free of guilt, and to free guilt. When Meister Eckhart said, "We pray to God to free us of God," he didn't put quotes around the second God, and never would have. This lies at the heart of his thinking—one word cannot be distinguished from itself. One word is always that one word. And the unsaying of a thought requires that the word used in the thought, right at the beginning, will not be distinguished from that word when it is reappraised, reused, or re-intended. God is one word that he prays we will be liberated from, because God cannot be reduced to the word God.

19. The language of translation, as Benjamin perceives it, is like poetic language because of its fusion of a literal reading of the word with the freedom of a second look. The contemporaneous moment involves just such a fusing.

20. Hans Jonas, in his great book *The Gnostic Tradition*, saw the links between ancient Gnostic thought and contemporary thought.

He wrote: "Dread as the soul's response to being-in-the-world is a recurrent theme in Gnostic literature. The world (not the alienation from it) must be overcome; and a world degraded to a power system can only be overcome through power. . . . Different as this is from modern man's power relation to the world-causality, an ontological similarity lies in the formal fact that the countering of power with power is the sole relation to the totality of nature left for man in both cases."

Modern warplanes that drop bombs on undefended people are material manifestations of ideas so overblown and mythic that there is no vocabulary on earth to respond to them. It is probably up to science to provide people with a new symbology that is modest enough to sustain our ardor for what exists.

21. We may not know if there is a God or not, but we do know that there is a word.

INCUBUS OF THE FORLORN

Thomas Hardy, who might be called "an incubus of the forlorn" after one of his own characters, and for whom the past is an obscure and heavy presence that folds each person into a path determined by probabilities and failures, suffered from his memories.

He might have wanted to purge them when he sat down to write. But he wrote, as all novelists do, backwards, in the body of a character entering the story with as much uncertainty as its author, and as if he had never been anywhere before.

He called his novels "imperfect little dramas of country life and passions." In them, he said he endeavored "to give shape and coherence to a series of seemings, or personal impressions." The word "seemings" rings a bell.

Seeming is a word applied to chance—What seems to be a chance occasion is an event that is only partially traceable through a larger evaporating scheme.

A chance meeting is a meeting that seems to exist with a great probability of *not* meeting circling around it.

As we all know, almost everything *doesn't* happen.

So the chance occurrence must actually be everything that does happen.

Hardy wrote about people failing to meet as if these failures are scandalous occasions. What didn't happen astounded him.

For some reason he wanted to know why two paths coming out of elsewhere and which converged still failed two people planning to meet there at a specific time.

Convergence—an appointment kept by two—for Hardy is the existential linchpin of his quest.

How can it happen and how can it not happen? If a person has said he will be in a certain place, shouldn't his body be as good as his word?

The fact is, once two have met, their meeting can never be erased from history.

The meeting may be minor, or major, in the emotional lives involved; but it has made an ineradicable place for itself in time.

The dread of an un-event, unwritten in time, haunted Hardy. It was a contradiction that held him inside literature—writing and history versus the unwritten in empty time. These became his subjects as much as his method.

Plot, which is twisted around the might-have-been and the how-it-was in equal measures, is any novelist's obsession.

But Hardy was rarely concerned with possibilities, which

suggest a range of potential changes in fortune spread out within reach. He saw his characters as socially limited and doomed to suffer from one disappointment after another and he made it clear that people were passive in relation to history; that historical forces acted upon individual temperaments like hands on wet clay.

It was as if he were saying, too, that a writer is molded by the imaginary or that characters are the little people of literature, midgets or slaves in the circus of the author's mind.

(Sometimes I think prostitution and slavery may be the actual subjects of all fiction because of the way fiction exploits its characters.)

Without the humiliation of social conventions in any written story, there is only a protection and reification of them by the plot.

Hardy circled around the effects of convention on people again and again; *Jude the Obscure* is Hardy's final revolution and it is relentlessly tragic.

(Convention, being structural, weirdly joins the unconscious in its control over the human impulses. Barely acknowledged, convention makes even love-talk a defense of its governance.)

While Hardy's stories became increasingly anguished in tone, he did not escape the tradition of his approach to narrative until he renounced the form entirely.

He referred to a plot as a scheme and charted detailed outlines before he began to write. As if he wanted to beat chance and to know exactly how everyone got where they were going.

Nonetheless, he said that the characters wrote the stories, and until they took over, he was uncomfortable with the work. Their blindness became his seeing, though they remained blind.

A path is like a plot—once formed, it seems to welcome and pull you into it. A path, while it is being made, offers itself, and obstacles too.

The path of entry into a novel is tangled but irresistible; it contains itself within an ever-diminishing scheme of probabilities and projections.

Is a moment predetermined or is it the result of a series of mental miscalculations?

The difficulty of decision-making hangs in this question, and plagues the storyteller.

Usually plot is to fiction what form is to poetry. It lifts and fills the rambling language and presses it down into a single shape and sound.

Poetry can be chance-generated, but fiction is always chance-generated although in an uncanny and dimly perceived way.

Characters often enter as ideas and exit as corpses.

Hardy's novels were like short stories in that they dealt with the lonely, unnoticed people in small villages around Dorset. He bore down on economics and psychology just as critically as Henry James did, but nature was his furniture and his art; it protected or exalted what was awful in the human.

+ + +

Hardy lived in the years when land was becoming *landscape*.

Forest, field, orchard, and small town life were rearranged in order to serve the economic needs of a few. That is, a landed bourgeoisie with ingratiating obedience to the aristocracies. These activities systematically ravaged the natural world where he grew up.

The nineteenth century landscape painting showed an England entirely tamed by its use-value.

The framed object (landscape) would soon become the film frame.

There are—in some of Thomas Hardy's novels—the signs of his poems coming, and of the necessity for film to be born as a great art form.

Hardy's exact descriptions of the natural world around Wessex where he grew up are devoted to storing up images of the wilderness before it is too late. His language speaks for the trees, apples, water, birds, hills; he writes what it is to be without a human anywhere around.

He was one of the last great describers, an occupation that film would soon take over. Like Gerard Manley Hopkins, he labored to make no distinction between words and natural things as sensual realities.

(At times his concern with specific angles of vision is a technique that also prefigures film.)

But primarily it is in the intensity of his depictions of the wild land around Wessex that his work becomes a forerunner to film.

In a sense the silence that film scores with music is the same white page that Hardy entered with words.

When a person, for the first time, picks up a movie camera and lets it roll over the surfaces, he or she confronts the intractable silence of the mouthless living. How can you make the hills talk back? What can you do with the opacity of a filmed image?

Because words can't be there, engorging the visible with meaning, music is often introduced instead of a new literature of image.

Hardy, who declared that he was "consigned to infelicity"—who could not make himself believe in or speak of God—stood with a notebook in the center of the natural world and described it as something that experienced itself as receding, calling, maintaining, shining. A place without a person. He saw the world the way we hope that the most attentive cameraperson will see, because then no speech or music will be necessary.

Why am I thinking of Hardy?

His men are my women, for one thing. In my novels, that is. His young male characters are bewildered and penniless, ethical and destroyed.

So in this sense, he is one of the last of the most recent novelists whose work I read as if they were written for me and my characters.

His absorption in the weathers of each day, the shapes of leaves and hills, their emotional contours, reflect some similar (New England) template buried in my brain.

Beyond that, I am at the end of a generation that began with existentialism; that still prefers irritation to irony; and that shares a political position sickened by the fatal incompatibilities between freedom and equality.

(Some of us still use old words like hope, luck, labor, and timing. We are unreconstructed but adaptable.)

We are not by any means done with the existentialism of Camus and Sartre, and we don't see the history of culture in blocks—as modernist one minute and postmodern the next—but as a long struggle without interruption.

The thinking of the fifties and sixties closed down like an old department store, abruptly and inexplicably, to make room for European cultural theory that entered with shiploads of prosperity and gloss.

But the same historical activity continued, following a centuries-old set of truths: absolute power corrupts and involuntary poverty corrupts if it can.

To return to Thomas Hardy is to glimpse a phantom prophet of the coming war-world that I grew up in.

The tenacious thrust of his novels, which one after another nailed down free-spirited characters onto the fates of their social bodies, still explains why the words "struggle" and "injustice" are knotted into economics.

His books show the close histories of laboring and uprooted people and support the resolutions of Marx and Engels.

Still, there is another reason why I love Thomas Hardy: because he finds no happiness in memory.

He can't execute a full-turn towards the past but is caught in one magnetic moment in time, where the eyes salt over, where what is lost is not yet radiant—not a joy but a source of deepest melancholy.

He writes as if he were ploughing a path from the wall to the gate. The future is always behind him.

Usually in his novels an idealistic laborer enters a village, perplexed and vulnerable, and develops intense desires that are invariably detoured by disappointment, missed appointments, and worldly incompetence. Sometimes there is a young woman who plays this role, and there is only one person weaker and more doomed than she, and that is her baby.

A common beginning goes like this: "One evening of late summer, before the present century had reached its thirtieth year, a young man and woman, the latter carrying a child, were approaching the large village of Weydon-Priors in Upper Wessex on foot."

Always the story seems to begin at the edge of a village, with someone either coming or going. There are, however, no margins or borders in Hardy's imagination, just as there are no "marginalized" people.

The life in the village is sufficient and central to itself.

And that center is everywhere the character is—rambler, worker, woman, landowner, snob.

Hardy always prefers one or two characters to the others, but he is fair to them all, which creates complications for the plot.

This sometimes results in one character peeking at another. Not on purpose, but because of timing, an accidental glimpse that turns into a prolonged pause. Peeking lets Hardy be in two places at once, and dispenses more innocence on people than they would otherwise be able to demonstrate. Peeking is like watching someone sleep. It is also like looking back in time and watching a movie.

The character with whom Hardy generally identifies the most is someone who enters his story uncorrupted. This character is subjected to experience—experience being anything that occurs as an outcome of necessity. Experience *is* necessity. For Hardy, the rest is calculation and malign excess.

He doesn't like the middle men or women, that great spread of settled society that sends out representatives to exploit the unsettled ones, because they are oblivious of the effects of their actions and of the reality of the people they are affecting.

In his novel *The Woodlanders* the thickening of a middle-class presence in a rural woodland village leads to a series of weak knocks, overhearings, misunderstandings, and bad timing.

The middle people err in relation to their interest in profit. They calculate their future on the basis of their own early experience with financial difficulty. This rules them, allows them to sell their own children in the name of security.

The unstable and uprooted people err in relation to their self-doubt and lowered sense of self-worth. A chain of disappointments has given them little reason to hope for success.

Probability is said to be expectation founded upon partial knowledge. It is determined by the frequency of an event occurring sequentially. Probability goes in both directions—towards past and future.

For example, I will probably make it from here to the door because I have done so before.

Probability becomes increasingly complex with the introduction of other people's feelings, sex, broken hearts, empathy, someone's unpredictability, and the development of mistrust.

If you had full knowledge, there would be no more probability, and you would see only a dull fractal consistency to the shapes of things and their paths.

But as it is, many people either foresee nothing but trouble ahead ("Danger—Heartbreak Ahead") or they refuse to see any trouble at all in case it will paralyze them.

(You feel yourself to be lost from sight only when you are intensely suffering.

For some, blessed by obscurity.

The more blessed, the more wobbly the borders between

parts, like the hair cut and sold, hair which is a thread from the head to the ethereal.)

The walls of a woman's womb contain the weakest living body, and in Hardy's stories there is often a miscarriage, or a child who dies. This event dispels all notions of margin, or border, because the air into which the weak extras fall is an air beyond experience.

An air of unrealized probabilities and untried survival.

A baby dies under the sign of lust alone, which is a blank.

Why else did the Church assign the ghosts of babies to Limbo where all is probable and nothing is tainted by having been?

The margins there are infinite. In Limbo dwell all those whom statistics leave out. Those who are not in heaven, not in hell, but somewhere hovering.

It is like a waste-field for the unexceptional, the undeveloped, the aborted and miscarried.

What happens in and to Limbo? Does it float around us? Do its souls ever escape from the possible into the good?

One fears the worst for those in Limbo—that they are outside of all attributes, unnamed, unclaimed, pure figures as transparent as glass, with nowhere to go.

Limbo is like a section of God—an invisible weight without boundaries. It exists in the range of consciousness; it holds what has slipped away, unnoticed. Like the half-formed cherubs emerging from clouds in paintings of the Annunciation, those in Limbo look happy about nothing.

+ + +

Babies died with their mothers, and alone, in large quantities until recently in the West, as they continue to do elsewhere around the world. They are banished to Limbo, then, where they wait for nothing, not even the Reckoning, because they have come from nothing in the way of experience.

Children in Hardy's novels seem to exist as probabilities, threats either in utero or near the central story, pulling characters into poverty. The presence of a child indicates a probable decline or disaster. The carrying of a child signals destitution.

One novel begins: "On an early winter afternoon, clear but cold, when the vegetable world was a weird multitude of skeletons through whose rise the sun shone freely, a gleaming landau came to a pause on the crest of a hill in Wessex."

In 1870, Hardy noted in his journal: "Mother's notion, and also mine: that a figure stands in our van with an arm uplifted, to knock us back from any prospect we indulge in as probable."

He took notes wherever he went, using the methodology of science that was becoming popular then. But he was always mesmerized by the blocked path, the road not taken. The action never made. The ghost of the lost became increasingly actual and threatening.

As a committed agnostic, he noticed that the war between body and soul is generally won by the body, which pleased him since he was himself an erotic thinker, who generally took the woman's part. He remembered women at the same time that he saw them.

Marty South, in *The Woodlanders*, is a young spar-maker by night and apple-picker and presser by day. Her one claim to beauty is her hair—whose abundance is "almost unmanageable . . . its true shade a rare and beautiful approximation to chestnut." A man wants to buy it from her to sell to a rich woman, and Mary says, "What belongs to me I keep." He compares how much she makes at her difficult day and night jobs with what she would get for her hair, and before long, she is persuaded, and she sells her hair.

This transaction corresponds to the destruction of the orchards and woodlands in the story surrounding Marty South. The selling of part of her body—her tumultuous and luminous hair—is the ultimate symbol of a person's renunciation to the profiteers moving in on the land.

If any good story illuminates these three areas of truth—the psychological, the sociopolitical and the existential—then Hardy accomplishes that in several of his novels. The act of turning a page—like lifting a veil—when reading Hardy is to participate in entering haunted, beautiful paths.

The un-manifested, the un-realized and dis-appointed suffer in the margins and out into the space surrounding the book. They circulate unexpressed, but possibly so close to actualization as to fill the consciousness of the reader with their presence.

When a choice enters a story it enters as a tiny trap more than an opportunity. Once the choice is made—"written in"—it can't be read as an error but as a fate. When the choice is influenced by casual moments—a storm, a letter blows away, or the face turns toward another; when the cruel words are uttered as easy speech or when the plan turns out to be an embarrassment—if it is now written in, it can't be written out.

None of us dares to say that a major choice we have made was a mistake.

We can't quite form such a judgment without fear. Instead, there is a retrospective accounting for all the contingencies that added up to the final selection.

Or we can do something that Hardy does.

We can see the whole sequence of events as always leading *away* from our arrival at the place where we really, originally wanted to be. We can see nothing but the absence of a progress; if anything, a circular turn, disruption, a raining down of distractions and misunderstandings.

The once-possible for a character becomes increasingly improbable.

The contradiction between the elusive and the trap is a contradiction inherent in story-writing itself.

How can something add up, when it is only conceived and then understood in reverse? By subtracting, until a lot of it is gone.

A tragic accident, for instance, means something terrible happened outside anyone's usual calculations. Even as you can go over every step that led to it—wishing you had chosen several other options during its progress—because it was never "probable," it cannot be adequately explained backwards.

You have to cut (or add) certain passages in order to make the accident seem probable.

An accident can't be added to the account without changing everything around it to make it look inevitable.

Otherwise an accident in a plot is like a lost page. It falls out of the book as a coincidence, or an act of God or Nature—earthquake, twister, shark, volcano, car crash, fiery explosion.

It splits and empties what was moving along systematically. It isn't fair.

It is this question of fairness that haunts the pages of a story.

It is what is meant by a good plot. It is what is intended by any writer who says a story finally works.

The characters have received equal time and equal attention (not necessarily in the amount of writing ascribed to them) and have passed through a series of scenes, interacting, with respect for the community of sentences as being both judgments and fates.

A social logic prevails. It can be read backwards and forwards seamlessly.

(But the world was unimaginably unfair in Hardy's mind.)

His skeptical novels are precursors of secular mid-twentieth century novels, perhaps the last best example of that tradition that lingered from the preceding century. While they tell us what it was like to live in nineteenth-century England and what kinds of failures and chances could redirect the course of an ordinary person's life when history imposed itself in sharp, spasmodic acts of destruction (industry), Hardy's pen is dipped in a metaphysical despair that Céline or Beckett would recognize.

His despair exceeds his subject, because it precedes it. He begins and stays at the half-turn, where, like a wounded angel, he has paused to look back and can't execute another move.

He reports on remorse. He reiterates the scene of the crime. He is mesmerized by it. A saturated landscape contains figures like the phantoms made of paint that trail across canvases.

The frame is immovable, the history closed on this "weather that the shepherd shuns."

Paradise may be the time when we can finally turn to our past and see that its beauty was there despite our being there. In fact, its beauty can finally be seen because we aren't there.

The purgatorial past is personal, it has your own smell and breath across it, and no matter how much you wish for the light to change, it stays gray and soaked in presence.

Old homes stare at you as if in a state of *unhope.*

"Spirit appears in Time, and it appears in Time just so long as it has not *grasped* its pure Notion, i.e., until it has annulled time. . . . Until Spirit has completed itself *in itself,* until it has completed itself as world-Spirit, it cannot reach its consummation as *self-conscious* Spirit." (Hegel)

+ + +

Fiction is concerned with victims of history, and the writer of fiction shares their plight by wrestling with the torturous clamp of plot. So plot traps the writer with his or her victims, just as history does.

What does it mean to finish writing a book?

It means that your plot has defeated you. You have been decimated by its logic, which is finally insufferable. It has worked its spell on you. You have to end the book and get some air.

Now you can measure the consequences of a choice made on page seven with its outcome on page eighty-seven, measuring it against a character's contingent and ambient relationships; measuring it against temperament, consistency of response, and likelihood of the ability to choose at all; measuring it against outside forces, historical, sociological, existential—these are the ways that make the medium of fiction also the message of its content.

This is no dream, no indulgence, no sentimentality, but the study of justice. And a struggle with the cold lock of history.

Hardy late in life stopped writing fiction entirely and turned to poetry, where he continued to hover at the place where "drops on gate-bars hang in a row."

PURGATORY & OTHER PLACES

In *Finnegans Wake* James Joyce set his long final narrative in Dublin's rains and ruins near the Vico Road that winds down to Killiney Bay and across Ireland to Purgatory where human errors fizzle into a hole.

In the thirteenth century Purgatory was discovered in Ireland; it was a hole in the ground on Station Island, near Donegal. There penitents were liberated from their sins.

This deep and insidious pit was also dubbed Saint Patrick's Purgatory.

Before this time there had been an actual geographic Earthly Paradise located in the East beside a four-branched river.

And for centuries there had been the dualistic associations of bliss with the sky and terror with the inside of the earth.

Mount Etna's volcanic basin was the location of Hell.

Manifestations of the divine cropped up in gardens, rock formations, and fire.

Martin Luther called Purgatory "the third place" and disapproved of its introduction into the study of theology.

Worldly Purgatory has been experienced as a penal colony, as a description of earthly existence—"first the sentence, then the verdict"—and as a hell of limited duration.

Life in Purgatory consists of a sequence of gestures and footsteps up a slippery circular cliff-side—each uneasy step bringing you closer to absolution and redemption in the face of God.

The Pseudo-Dionysius wrote of an intelligence that circles the truth: "the knowledge of divine things illuminates it; not by way of intuition or in unity, but thanks to discursive reasons and, so to speak, by complex and progressive steps."

Purgatory consists of a sequence of difficult movements that spring from a yearning for liberation from those movements. There is something about this joke that is familiar.

For one thing, the idea of Purgatory evolved at the same time as legal theory, secular and canonical. Complex categories for crime and punishment were concocted, analyzed, and named by theologians and government officials together while Purgatory entered the theological map as an official site.

Sins, venial and mortal, forms of guilt, and methods of contrition multiplied alongside investigations into psychology and intention.

Mathematics and spiritual progress worked in tandem. Both time and space were peppered with accounts, how many acts would release how much sin, how many prayers would erase how much guilt.

The little progress called *Saint Patrick's Purgatory* was a bestseller in the Middle Ages. It was written around 1200 A.D. by a Cistercian monk—H of Saltrey—who repeated the story of someone who had endured the physical ordeals of being thrown into that actual pit.

When the hero was about to be given his freedom, he was told: "There is no way for those who are being tortured to know how long they will remain in the penal palaces, because their trials can only be alleviated by means of masses, prayers, and alms given on their behalf."

And in a vision the Emperor Charles the Fat hears his father, Louis the German, speak to him from a vat of boiling water which comes up to his knees. He stands there and tells his son not to worry. He is in purgatory where scores are made even.

"I spend," he explains, "one day in this basin of boiling water, but the next day I am transported into that other basin, in which the water is very cold."

Beckett wrote: "On this earth that *is* Purgatory, Vice and Virtue—which you may take to mean any pair of large contrary human factors—must in turn be purged down to spirits of rebelliousness."

Dante read H of Saltrey's popular pamphlet, but Beckett noted that Dante placed his paradise above in invisible spheres, and Joyce placed his at "the tradesman's entrance to the seashore."

+ + +

The Israelites burned their way into a future across the desert and towards a region which was stony or ready for vineyards. It is called the Promised Land—home, where there is at least hope for justice and sanctuary.

Ireland for Joyce was not the Promised Land by a long stretch; rather, it was a penitentiary afloat, stones and sins locked in a stone-colored sea. It was more a trial than an isle. When he left it, he flew from his sentence as if towards paradise. In exile, he wrote his progress often in the voice of a woman.

When Anna Livia spoke of her birth, she might have been describing coming downstairs into a household.

"I was sweet when I came down out of me mother. My great blue bedroom, the air so quiet, scarce a cloud. In peace and silence. I could have stayed up there for always only. It's something fails us. First we feel. Then we fall. And let her rain now if she likes."

The failing, the falling, and the landing under the rain, at home in Dublin.

In exile you are circled by lands that are not just unknown but alien to you, and weathers that are often menacing because they lack any corresponding climate from your own past.

+ + +

You are unable to read the landscape as a recognizable face. Instead you ride the bone and flesh of it like a fly.

To choose to leave home is one thing. To be forced—by political or economic realities—is another. If you have to leave home and inhabit a place where you don't want to be, you reach the very lowest point in uncertainty.

For many people, placing all their attention on acclimatizing their children to the new place is the way they act for their own survival; the children become envoys and shields and the parents work so that the children, not they, can become socialized to both the people and the landscape where they have arrived.

If you go into exile alone, without a companion or child, the landscape remains hostile and nauseating. The hills and highways are emblematic of a purgatorial God-empty fate. What if we named certain places on earth after their metaphysical properties? For instance, what if a penitentiary was called Federal Exile or State Purgatory?

There is such a place in a town in California called Pleasanton.

It is a city of gray bar motels about forty-five miles east of Oakland. Pleasanton includes—besides its many kinds of prisons—fast chicken, burger, coke, gas, and taco joints and islands of manicured housing units, even some ritzy properties bundled up in trees and shrubs, out beyond the grim penitential structures.

It all seems of a piece, a sample of whole-cloth, the seamless tapestry of brown fields beyond the Central Valley—with birdish windmills hardly moving—with warnings of wind and dust storm—leading to this prison city.

That the area housing Camp Parks—a Federal facility—should be named Dublin may be even more bizarre than a prison city called Pleasanton.

But there it is, Dublin. And inside it Camp Parks seems as deserted as everywhere else around, like a military base that has been vacated because of a leak in its nuclear arsenal, so you follow the glitter of cars in a tarmac park and see the looped, spiked wiring over high fencing.

And you know you are near the person you are visiting—one woman among hundreds locked up here.

Check-in is lonely, a passage back and forth through an electronic arch, with others doing the same, the abandonment of all personal articles at the desk, a signing-in, and then a temporary halt inside vaulted doors before admission into Camp Parks and the cafeteria area where your friend (Marilyn Buck) will meet with you.

Women prisoners are already there, several being visited by men, children, parents, and friends, all dressed casually, coolly, due to the heat.

There are vending machines, soda cans on tables, a place for small children to play, an outdoor cement patch to sit on with a few flowers planted there, female guards clanking with keys.

The view to the outdoors is built to allow no entrance for memory.

The wiring, the fencing, the concrete.

The place is the antithesis of the changeability of social action and nature's motion.

Because women are the ones who live here, there is a lot of business around food and children. Popping of cans, ripping of candies, playfulness. But because every step is a baby step and there is no measuring of steps anywhere else, the moral arc of this universe tends towards stasis.

You want to ask "How did you get here?"

And then you want to ask "How can you bear it?"

You really want to know what lies behind the steel door with the light that radiates red when a prisoner is ready to be released into the cafeteria.

Many women have been brought here on drug charges. Some are in for life having refused to snitch on a boyfriend. Many are inside for decades though they never committed a violent act.

Their children and grandchildren visit and depart.

Some are "domestic terrorists" and will never be released in time to live reasonably youthful lives in the world.

There are political prisoners—some of them former Black Panthers—who have been incarcerated for more than twenty years. There are more recent ones, who will be here indefinitely, including the MOVE family survivors. Women.

Some of the women here were involved in violent acts; others were not; but they all share belief in a real enemy.

So what is such an enemy?

Someone who has contempt for your fear of him and who, at the same time, will kill you if you overcome your fear and fight him.

+ + +

The end result is that you spend your time protecting your fear, making sure it is hidden.

In such a way the problem of identity is different here than anywhere else; your true identity is your hidden self, not the persona you show to the world.

This is where self-censorship enters and purgatory begins.

You don't allow yourself to think certain thoughts, to glance in certain directions, to move a certain way.

Women are sentenced to fifty or a hundred years for weapons possession and political affiliation, for drug possession, and for resistance by silence.

Three to a cell. Days monitored down to a minute.

No time, no privacy. Whispers. Strip searches and physical surveillance.

Outside the misty California sky lies low. The low-slung buildings have an aura that is so heavy, the place seems like a holy place.

And birds, bees, flowers, and trees seem to live in the deep dream state as our enduring witnesses to bliss. A person dies into that state as one occasionally sleeps in it, forgetful of all, the body thrown down like an offering, the "spirit purged and fit to ascend to Heaven."

CATHOLIC

What can you do after Easter?

Every turn of the tire is a still point on the freeway.

If you stand in one, and notice what is all around you, it is a pile-up of the permanent.

The churn of creation is a constant upward and downward action; simultaneous, eternal.

If you keep thinking there is only an ahead and a behind, you are missing the side-to-side which gives evidence to the lie that you are moving progressively.

If everything is moving at the same time, nothing is moving at all.

Time is more like a failed resurrection than a measure of passage.

2.

The drive from the I-5 along Melrose to Sycamore.

The drive up La Brea to Franklin and right then left up to Mulholland.

The drive along Santa Monica to the rise up to the right and Sunset.

The drive along Sunset east past the billboard of the man on a saddle.

The drive from the 405 up onto La Cienega and the view of hills.

The difference between nirvana and nihil.

3.

Thomas Aquinas was an itinerant thinker. His thinking rolled like a reel.

It went forwards as a movement backwards. His thoughts may have been placed on the side like the eyes of many intelligent animals.

To mitigate pain he recommended weeping, condolence by friends, bathing, sleep, and contemplation of the truth.

He was the ninth of nine children and was sent very early to a monastery. The Dominicans luckily had no rule about staying in one place. So he could walk from city to city in Italy.

4.

Legal thoughts were developed by the Dominicans when they were assigned the job of creating penitential acts that matched each sin. They had to study humanity closely and seriously. Thomas took on this task as it became his life-work, his Summa, his body of words that he called straw in the end. Something to burn.

5.

Human nature: what is it?

The source and the destiny of each life are the same: an unknown that is unknowable. Unknown before; around and unknown now; and unknown after unless already fully known before.

Every act and thought has to be measured against this that has no limits. Why?

Because the failure to grow and flourish and develop is a terror; to die prematurely without having found any consolation for disappointment is an injustice.
A person wants to be known, to add up, to be necessary.
The only way to assure that this can happen is for there to be a way to study each action in relation to its immediate objective and to its surrounding circumstance: who, what, where, by what ends, why, how, when. You can by these terms measure your action in the world, but its final objective remains the same: unknown.

6.

For some persons, meditation, contemplation, prayer indicate that there is an emptiness already built into each body and it is that which (paradoxically) makes them feel at home in the cosmos.

7.

For others the hoarding of capital signals a loss of desire for any more knowing; it substitutes numbers for information. It creates a safety net out of figures.

8.

The taste and smell of an action, any action, comes from its objective. This is the strange thing about relationship. What you desire is what creates your quality. You are not made by yourself, but by the thing that you want. It is that sense of a mutually seductive world that an itinerant life provides. Because you are always watching and entering, your interest in fixtures grows weary and your strongest tie is to the stuff off to the side traveling with you.

9.

Lemon-water light of California. Flattened with big boulevards and wandering men and women depleted at bus stops. Back alley bungalows. A terry cloth sash, evidence of neglect.

10.

The walk up Sycamore at night with Tom, looking in lighted windows and at varied architectures, Mediterranean and Mexican. The warm night's pungent gas fume and flower.
Nights alone on Sycamore, grown children gone, windows open, bars and screens, my silver screen darting images onto my shirt.

+ + +

The drive down La Brea at dawn to get on to the San Diego freeway with trucks and commuters catching the Stock Market opening in NYC. The lineaments of daybreak are silken tar and stars.
Traffic is already on hard and Boston early morning news.

11.

Passions are eliminations, but they are critical to the body's survival, because they attract, command, and absorb; they make vig-
ilant. Hope and fear, these are the two passions that loom behind
all the others. I know a man driven by fear, and another one
deluded by hope.

12.

Pain interferes with your ability to concentrate. A priest told me
to prepare for the end while I am still mentally ordered. Old age
can scatter the work of a lifetime. Probably people should go
Sannyasa as soon as they retire, and become wanderers, contem-
platives, ones who act charitably all the day long.

13.

An ethics of intentionality must stay at a practical, measurable
level, and never become abstract. Don't ever argue principles,
my father told me. Stay with the facts.

14.

These scribbles? Stray ends? Ardor's droppings?
Illness has its own aura. And one who adores haloes can smell and
see the aura of illness.
A thick swimmer. Through the door, an odor.
A mystifying sniff. Millions of them worldwide.
Geese are going over, raw as a jet stream, the windows open and
a stick finger plunged into a science jar. Seedless.

Nature exists in a deep sleep, Eden's sleep. This is why watching
and hearing the wind in the trees or the waves brings such peace.
If Natural Light is the imprint of Divine Light, the word Divine
is unnecessary.

15.

In some form or other, the deformity of the form is always potential as opposed to immanent. Perfection requires attention.

16.

Asshole or jerk? Which one gets to be President.

You know the man by the punishment he deserves and doesn't
get.
He can actually perfect his sin with malicious intent and no one
will even notice.
Because we have an infinite disposition for wanting the good.

17.

The freeway passes the airport and its glut of traffic, the planes' bellies ballooning over the lines of cars. Bullets and bombs and parachutes ghost and worm their way out of them to cover the head. South lies ahead and more south, an opening to the sky bending down like the head of a lamb. I like the look of a mountain.
Mine eyes see the sun rising from mine east, they often have tears in them that will soon be blinding and blessing at the same time. Long Beach and oil and electricity and the military built all the way to the beach—their forms the forms of insects who are empty of sleep.

Hills and fields around Irvine and the Lagunas. Fieldworkers bent over green and white. Now is the time for the Sixth International Brigade.

As I get older I don't remember what things are, only what they look like and are named. The way Los Angeles becomes hell at night after being purgatorial all day.
When allegory enters time, it is the sign of profound danger.

18.

The Dominicans, a young order, were given the task of instructing others in penances. Therefore, the study of human nature was critical. They soon found out that studying human action was the same as studying God and creation. Aquinas went on to discover that all labor is study of the divine since the divine is everything and anyone who lives is stuck inside the structure of God the Cosmos. He was concerned with being, not doing. And his love for the world was so intense, it infused his thought with compassion for all things. He has been compared to Confucius, Sankara, phenomenology. He makes it possible for some people now to remain Catholic despite enormous misgivings and consciousness of the Church's bad acts. He's not the only one who makes it possible, but he is an important one because he is still considered an Angelic Doctor of the Church, one whose thought remains foundational in Catholicism. You can find his mind there, waiting, permitting, guiding right into modern-day life. He saw each person as an important piece of a magnificent puzzle made by and for God.

Plummet into that mystery if you want to know more.

19.

Aquinas walked until he banged into a tree, and then he collapsed and died soon after. He didn't want to write another line anyway. Modest and bewildered until the end. He never stopped equating joy with truth.

20.

I can't believe I can see. I can't believe I can hear. I can't believe I can speak or think. What are commodities but evidence of lost people. You cannot love a bathrobe so what can you love about your own texture.

21.

The airplanes' bellies and bonnets loom over the freeway landing at LAX. Ahead is south of south, Irvine, an opening to distance. I like the look of a mountain of matter.

22.

The hills plunge down to the Pacific that I forgot to view. Six a.m. en route to work. Deepening as the sun warms and lifts. Rev and veer and avoid exits at all costs. Rows of settlements will deteriorate, designed to fall lightly flat in an earthquake.

23.

Every turn of the tire stops at a halfway point to nothing, Parmenides. To walk this walk would be better, to walk from Sycamore Street to La Jolla.

One hundred miles.
The only end sought for in itself is the last end. It is always present in us, after, after. The sky all around.
The completion of ourselves.

24.

Evil is the privation of good in any subject, it is a weakness and a lack. This is why it is compatible with capital.
It may lack reason, or heart, or conscience, or empathy, it is a sign of incompletion, it is an exaggeration of one quality at the ex-

pense of others that must be banished in order for that one to thrive.

Intention is hardly distinguishable from morality. It colors the action that comes from it with the shade of the desired end. The sad thing is that you can apprehend your goal as good and be wrong. Most of the time this is what happens and so you have the problem of judging yourself in terms of both intention and desired end, when things go wrong.

2 5.

Where did I go wrong? At the same place everyone else did?

Why did I end up living in unhappiness for so many years? Unhappiness was the desert, literally and figuratively.

Trees that don't move. Sun on dry dog turds. Black immobile shadows. Temporary infinity.

This was not home because my interior landscape was composed of wet, watery images—soggy brick, flowerpots, begonias, big morning glories, sloppy roads, and turbulent skies. But something worse, generally, was occurring in the world around me, as it also occurred to me. The restlessness, the consciousness of a disappearing base and goal, the lack of home and civic engagement. I loved no city that I recognized.

Anything can happen under these conditions. Nuclear bombs, dirty bombs, small-time random murder and abduction.

26.

At the Marine training base, the second border of Mexico begins, call it San Diego County. The twin-breasted nuclear power plant beside the pap-white sea. America stops here.

America is not located in the small beads of sand, the pelicans, dolphins, or the arching erotic hills. Fish tacos and a woman driving alone at dawn with immigrants packed inside the truck ahead of her.
We have left America to the conceptual capitalists.
But so-called Americans have settled here, as on the West Bank of Israel where cheap housing for U.S. Christians is expanding.

27.

A train runs parallel to its tracks and the freeway.
Eucalyptus borders the road through Leucadia along the tracks, heading south, the lettuce melting in the boxcars like a poor film sequence.
The second border on the other side of the freeway crossing north at the Marine training base. Ugly nuclear power plants, the humping hills.

Women running alone at dawn, aliens sending money home, in their wallets pictures of family and friends, love letters, addresses, I don't want to be here.
The canyons are groomed and pocked with bourgeois housing developments that are built for eclipse. The spirit muscles its way

out of disappointment and follows the body laughing. Jesus after Easter is laughing all the way down the road.

Tramps, boxcars, Marx, tacos, Dos Equis, rabbits uprooted and fobbed onto parks, coyotes splitting into lonely wanderers, tractors, tanks, and brutalist walls. "This is the future," said a professor. The ocean forms a raised screen at the end of every west-side road. Strange how it lifts like that. Mustard carpeting the canyons.

28.

Night drive along Mission Blvd., left on Turquoise to get to the 5 south. Happy stop-offs, proximate ends, promised lands, ruthless and armed RVs beside chugging little geezers. Old Town to exit on Washington and up dazzled adobe trash to see the east out of a plate-glass window on Georgia, then back to Normal Street for chicken.

I am West or something. I don't know, but night clouds roll out of the east as voluminous pitch that erases the stars.
I love being awake, someone said of her insomnia. She hid the night in her closets and left the rest in color.

So nature remains but grace passes like a panopticon flowing its light onto others in its slow circular motion.
Fugitive soul of the battered woman. She keeps running in search of a safe-shaped geography. It could be as flat as the desert. You are obliged to follow your reason, even helter skelter through the canyons. You are obliged because there is inside you a living soul that fears annihilation before happiness can discover it.

29.

If something you do is good for more people than you yourself, you can be pretty sure it is the right thing. (That is, it will make you happy.)

Speed, aptitude, certitude. Direct yourself towards action. It is imperative to find a virtue in itinerancy because this is the world now. People are either fugitives who want to go home, or seekers who don't want to go home. The movement of immigrants across borders brings much suicide with it. Imperiled people give birth to more children than people who are settled and comfortable. The success of rabbits.

Sorrow weighs down your brain with water.

30.

All hope depends on possibility. But you can't have hope outside of an immediate, active concern for justice; and this complicates the processes.

Aquinas set out to prove that what we seek is actually what we are already.

This thought requires more thought. Another way of putting it is: When Aquinas equates God with happiness, we know what he means by happiness.

31.

The Egyptian women lied in order to protect the babies of the Hebrew women. God rewarded them for their lie. He gave them houses on earth. Moral ethicists are disturbed by this hypocrisy on God's part. But this is one way the notion of "person" is born. How is it lost?

32.

The intellect is contemplative.
Voluntary ignorance is a terrible social sin.
The embrace between faraway, freeway, and very near is air, breath, oil, here.
Mouth and food. Going somewhere you don't want to be. How does the will work. I don't want to go where I am going!
Peripatetic effusions.

33.

I pretend I trust surface truths, that I am moving forward, street by street, and everything I pass, is passed. I have a goal, a plan, and I receive what comes to me in the form of smell, sight, touch, sound.
The street that I can't see exists now in a state that will receive me as I enter it and everyone else will enter the next moment at the same moment I do. The world is round and I am walking it. Time is space.
I pretend that I can take a step, with D—th directing traffic and earthquake and heartbeat and hate, is all I know of faith.

Doubt allows God to live.

34.

Sometimes you are privileged with a glimpse of the other world, when the light shines up from the west as the sun sets and dazzles something wet. The world is just water and light, a slide show through which your spirit glides.

Reason is the dominant weapon of oppression. (Reason versus Person.)
Reason without the other values becomes evil.
Reason where it just lodges in me as an anonymous individual is still oppressive but it works best in harmony with other passions—people are depending on me is the main one.

But if I were president, I would reason the world into horrific war because I would not let myself feel compassion or hope. I would eliminate passions that contradicted my reason.

35.

Plato believed that criminals wanted punishment. In a sense they committed the crime in order to suffer for having thought up an evil in the first place. The crime was the proof of a worse evil: the mental plan. The crime allowed them to be punished for an intention.

In the same sense Aquinas knew that thought was contaminated, but he took circumstances into account and was not a judgmental kind of man, but he didn't have much truck with morose delectation, that kind of morbid indulgence in painful thoughts. Why, because they really undermine hope.

36.

I once spent a night near Massachusetts Bay, near Boston, Quincy graveyard, and home. I don't know why I agreed to this, because it was something I didn't want to do. I felt sorry for the person who asked me, and no wonder. She was a tramp with severe medical problems. She had been given a couch to sleep on for one night and wanted me to sleep on a thin bed upstairs. She didn't care about me. Now I realize that I did it because I wanted to know where the ground of being weakens.
I think you can know more if you do things that are fearful or unpleasant, as long as they do not include hospitals or jails.

Wanting to know is what makes me do things I don't want to do. Wanting to know how far I can go with what I know.

37.

This is why I keep moving and only stop for the Eucharist in a church where there are sick, vomiting, maimed, screaming, destroyed, violent, useless, happy, pious, fraudulent, hypocritical, lying, thieving, hating, drunk, rich, poverty-stricken people.

WORK AND LOVE

I once made a short video about Simone Weil. I went to the church she had attended—Corpus Christi—when she lived in New York in 1942. My camcorder was an early model Sony, heavy and cheap. Thus far I had only practiced on random shoots that were both amateurish and conventional.

When I looked, much later, at the imagery my camera had collected, I saw a series of chess squares. Yellow light through square glass infused the space with a honey tone. A black and white checkerboard floor. The same floor appeared in a religious painting over the altar but I only noticed that later on screen.

The church floor, the church windows, the pavement in the park outside—all squares.

I remembered my dream of the night before: I was clumsily sewing a sampler out of earth colors.

Birds and branches were the images I wanted to make. But it was sloppy and ugly work when it was done.

Then I turned the cloth over. On the other side was a delicate and perfectly formed tapestry of flowers, twigs, and little birds.

Driving that day I saw a landscape that was strangely like a span of lifetime. Nothing special, but a spread of gray hills and highway. The world seemed flat and the sky an empty convex mirror.

Does something mechanical like a camera teach its user how it works? It feels as if it knows more than I do all the time because it contains the collective intelligence of the people who made it.

I decided to stay at the most trusting level with this film and let it emerge from what was given to me, and what I could afford.

An aesthetic based in poverty? The meaning of voluntary poverty in liberation theology is nonattachment to material goods and a resistance to exerting one's power over the natural world and other people.

A literature made out of light, lit from itself, ignited by electrical currents; this should cost very little.

Because it was summer, I had time off from my job. So I took a pile of children and went to stay on an island.

Large raindrops spattered on tile and asphalt.

The white light of a sky lit from behind, milky. Grass growing from sand and glass too.

I was waiting for someone who once loved me, and the silence had become a force.

Silence seemed to collaborate with the person who didn't appear and wouldn't.

The silence acquired a presence over the days. It reminded me that it was the love I missed more than the whole person.

"The First Life has forgotten me and the Second does not inquire after me," the Mandaeans wrote.

I remember, as a child during the Second World War, times when silence was a bodily presence, a field of light that eluded me. And even then I was praying and praying for someone to return who didn't, at least not for a long time.

In those years the movies showed news clips before each film: images of soldiers' corpses, prisoners of war, mass graves, and terrified civilians. Bodies and their faces on screen seemed to have risen from the grave, witnessing their own predicament too late to be of any use.

Curling strips of film were as luminous as a sidewalk in the rain, their transparency and texture thrilling; for me, emerging into the Cold War, projected silver film would always represent the language of the deceased.

The great filmmaker Robert Bresson wrote: "My movie is born first in my head, dies on paper, is resuscitated by the living persons and real objects I use, which are killed on film but, placed in a certain order and projected onto a screen, come to life again like flowers in water."

There is an ultimacy about a film splattered with white light and darting static, where the images are pale gray and the subtitles fade into white inventing a new poetry.

+ + +

Inside a camera the image reverses as it passes through you and your eyes and out again. The camera does all the work but it feels like a baby's head on your arm.

Does a baby's head contain all the knowledge of the cosmos it will ever need? And only waits for the tools to find it?

I have read SW for so long, and so intensely, I often don't remember what she believed, stated, or knew. In a sense my stupidity is a sign that I have incorporated her work into myself.

The more information I have, the less I can remember.

Someone said that because Blake was self-educated, he was smart one moment and childish the next. And also that he acted as if no one else had ever thought the same things he did.

I realized I wouldn't be able to afford to go to Paris or Marseilles to take pictures of places where SW had spent significant time. I would have to work within a budget that would decide the outcome of the project. I would only be able to include, on this video, the New York and London periods in her life.

At that time (1942) she was in exile from France. Extreme homesickness contributed to her final illness.

People are repelled by her loss of will at the end, but war can make people sick and defeat them even if they aren't stuck right in it.

During wars fought in the Middle East (Desert Storm, Eternal

Justice) a number of us experienced them as absurd slaughters for which we felt responsible, and got sick.

Blake wrote, "I was in a Printing house in Hell and saw the method in which knowledge is transmitted from generation to generation."

In early September I went to London where I filmed in Holland Park, near Simone Weil's last residence when she was ill and dying. It was a wasted day. The pictures from the park were meaningless, and I thought one house was hers but it wasn't.

The park was ragged, with dusty roads and short wooden fencing. It was bordered by a very ritzy neighborhood.

The weather was warm, the feeling reminiscent of Washington, D.C. Renovated townhouses and gardens in front and behind.

Every move I made was an error.

Next I filmed at Hyde Park where I knew SW often went on Sundays. The Kensington Gardens were thick with tall flowers, fountains, and herbs. Everything there was suffused with a sweetness and lavender light.

I spent a long time there wandering and thinking of her, growing ill, with German bombs exploding in the neighborhood. It was leafy and autumnal.

Still fine weather the next day. I went to film SW's last residence, the right one this time, at 31 Portland Road. The streets were narrow and on Pottery Lane I found the Church of St. Francis of Assisi, which she attended and where I sat for a while.

I filmed her house, front and back.

I filmed sidewalk emblems in a sort of moist and autumnal atmosphere.

As usual, in my solitude, I wondered what I was doing anywhere, although I knew I had to be somewhere as long as I was alive.

I was used to writing, but what would editing a video be like?

I had scrawled into my notebook these lines by a Jewish mystic (who?) about the way to achieve an insight: "If it be night, kindle many lights, until all be bright. Then take ink, pen, and a table to thy hand and remember that thou art about to serve God in the joy of the gladness of thy heart. . . . Now begin to combine a few or many letters, to permute and to combine them until thy heart be warm. . . . Then be mindful of their movements and of what thou canst bring forth by moving them. . . . And when thou feelest that thy heart is already warm and when thou seest that by combinations of letters thou canst grasp new things which by human tradition or by thyself thou wouldst not be able to know and when thou art thus prepared to receive the influx of divine power which flows into thee, then turn all thy true thought to image the Name."

Strangely this statement corresponds to some of Weil's thoughts about labor and how all our work should be directed towards the good.

In the legend of the ring of Gyges, which she liked, a man discovers a magic ring in the belly of a horse lying inside a cave. Whenever he puts the ring on his finger, he disappears. This way he can gain easy access to secret information and women inside the castle; he can become rich; he can wield power. He does all of these.

This legend has been quoted to explain the first human experience with money; it also has shown that the person who has power is usually invisible.

As long as money is understood only by those who have studied economics, there is little chance that its unreality for the rest of us will end.

This is why, to the contemporary worker, there can be no logical connection between work and pay.

Paid for what?

I am paid to be docile, to perform a random function all day without protesting.

Slaves modernized most of the farm equipment they were using because they were so familiar with its weaknesses. Even now people who do difficult and dangerous work get paid less than those who sit in front of a computer or talk on the phone all day.

But it is the least noticed person in the hierarchy who has the best knowledge of what is wrong with the hierarchy.

And it is the person who resists it all by being disreputable and elusive who doesn't get paid for anything and is more invisible than those who have power.

I went to Mass at the Church of St. Francis of Assisi, he who wrote, "While you proclaim peace with your lips be careful to have it more fully in your heart."

It was the last day of shooting. My daughters and their friends picked me up in their jalopy. I stuffed our picnic in the trunk.

This was the most momentous day in the whole project.

We were going to Ashford in Kent, where Simone Weil was buried.

I had packed hardboiled eggs, cheeses, lettuce, tomatoes, pita bread, Irish bread, wine, beer, water, and chocolate biscuits.

London seemed to stretch as far as Los Angeles. The sky was high and blue the way it is in America. Revolutionary music played on the car radio.

On the highway at last, the car broke down.

We waited patiently for a tow truck. B said he believed SW was now in control, and the timing was in her hands, and pilgrimages are notoriously filled with obstacles.

The driver of the tow truck was named Money. He was big and good-natured.

He dropped us near a train station and went away with the car, and we traveled back and forth on local trains free, trying to wend our way in the direction of Ashford.

At one station the conductor was young and new to the job and almost put us on the wrong train, and I began to panic. The sky was deepening, the shadows lengthening, and two children in wheelchairs were deposited and weirdly abandoned on the railroad platform.

The little boy had to pee and so the kindly conductor took him to the toilet. The little girl, pale and twisted and frightened, told us her name was Josephine. She wanted to keep us with her by talking. So B conversed with her until the train came. Then we had to leave her alone on the platform. She was crying as we rolled away. Why was she there alone, we wondered. Should we have left her behind?

I took pictures out the window of the train, shooting in the direction of Ashford. It was farther than any of us had imagined, and I had time to think now of Weil's last journey to the sanitarium out here—it was a hospital for industrial workers—and she was dying of bad lungs, starvation, and depression. But a friend of hers had recalled that she was happy to be in the country and people visited her there.

Ashford looked ultra-bourgeois and used up in the encroaching twilight.

We didn't know how to find the cemetery; it had been referred to as "the new Catholic cemetery" and the cab driver didn't know what that could mean, but took us to a Catholic church to find out. The priest was gone.

Then I mentioned the name of the hospital, Middlesex, where she had stayed before coming here, and the cab driver said we might be in the wrong Ashford. There was another one only an hour outside of London and it was in Middlesex!

He dropped us off at a very old ruined cemetery, where we wandered in a frenzy of doubt while the sky grew darker.

Starlings mobbed the trees and made an irritating racket. I took some random pictures and we drifted up the side of a busy highway in the direction of another graveyard the cab driver had mentioned. By now my daughters were convinced that I had made a huge blunder and so was I.

Then, rounding a corner, we saw a big sign: SIMONE WEIL AVENUE.

A memorial plaque donated by the French government hung on a wall.

We ran, it was 7 P.M. and Byebrook Cemetery was behind the police academy, just off that highway. All I remembered from one biography was that her grave was in the third row away from a hedge in the Catholic section.

The graves here were new, dating mostly from the war, and we found at the back a couple of rows of stones with Irish and Polish names inscribed on them; it was obviously the Catholic section.

The sky was blood orange by now and the trees pointy and bird-shrill. We split apart and tore through the gloaming, and at 7:30 my daughters found her grave. A flat square pressed into the ground, nearly invisible, circled by hawthorn ripped apart by the wind, with a few pink blossoms hanging on. A bunch of plastic carnations in French tricolors. Her grave lay halfway between the Catholic and Jewish sections of the cemetery.

We buried a flower bulb and a stone I had carried from the Irish Sea, and B poured French Vittel water around the hawthorn.

The sky was a splendid deep apricot color and it was all but night. The utter obscurity of the place, at this most obscure hour of the day, to me was true to the intentions of her life.

Weeks later, viewing the footage I had collected, I saw that her flat stone was cut to the size of the pavement that I had filmed all around her house in London. The checkerboard motif had continued in my camera throughout the trip. I had not been aware of it while I was shooting.

It would take several months to edit the footage, to write the script, and to select the music. I kept a log of hundreds of shots, many taken on the island, some in my own apartment, some from London and New York.

First came the choosing of images that in themselves had a kind of radiance and integration. Then I had to toss out many of them because they didn't fit into the larger plan. Then came the discovery of the script; it was a section from one of her notebooks, called "Prologue." Then came the selecting and sequencing of the good images, so that they blended on impact—because of color, shape, size, or movement—in relation to the written script. This was almost identical to the process of writing a poem or a good paragraph. Finally, the music—Shostakovitch.

I am aware that there is a vision of a just world behind language, sentences, syllables.

The evolution of a single word, into syllable, sound, amendment, assertion, tends towards justice. In every sentence you take measure of all the words in relation to each other.

Qualifying elements, adjectives that must never be excessive or unfair to the others.

Edward Dahlberg was right when he insisted on an ethics of composition.

But what about working with images? Would that process be equivalent?

The quest for just proportions—was this a quest for a kind of crushing coherence and cohesion, the way a piano piece can ultimately implode its lyricism into a single new sound?

As it turned out, editing the video was very much the same process. I disappeared into the little darkroom just as I approached a bunch of papers on my table. The fact is, whatever one person does, it is always only that person doing it. To spend a great deal of time seeking a form that is right for you is a waste. It will always only be you with whatever you are doing.

I expected the film to run about fifteen minutes. It ran twelve. And it took at least that many months to edit it with the help of others at my job.

In the end the filmmaker Babette Mangolte read the voice-over, and she told me how I should have made the video, beginning with the writing and ending with the filming.

She made it clear that I had done the whole process backwards.

Once I went to visit Simone Weil's close friend Simone Dietz, who lived in a high-rise old people's home overlooking the Massachusetts Turnpike in Springfield. She had worked for the Red Cross during the war and had been close to Weil in New York City in 1942, and then in London where they traveled together to work for the war effort.

Dietz was a woman without guile, and had no interest in idealizing Simone Weil or cashing in on the friendship. Several times she said that her friend would have been appalled by the seriousness with which her words were being taken, since she had never edited or amended the notebooks which have become the substance of her influence.

Simone Dietz was very overweight, with thick glasses and a piercing intelligence. She sat in a wheelchair half-blind in this high-rise building, her bed weighted with books on theology and philosophy and she watched daily Mass on television. She was a longtime convert from Judaism to Catholicism and once went to Lourdes, where she was carried up by Mary, who looked as she does in the Greek ikons. She was mortified by this experience, and hated to speak of it.

She told me that during the year in New York, Weil had dragged her to churches in Harlem, where she joined in with the clapping and jumping of the congregation.

She said the food-hating Weil ate hardly anything when she was at home. But she ate well at the Dietz apartment.

She said Mme. Weil was very powerful and terrified her husband, a doctor, who should have stopped Simone from returning to London since she obviously had tuberculosis.

Weil apparently had a very nasal voice, and believed herself to be hideous. The reason she could talk so freely to Father Perrin was that he was blind. She was always afraid of hurting his feelings, though, with her harsh critique of Catholicism.

At the same time, Weil would never speak to Jacques Maritain, because of his views on Greek slavery.

+ + +

Once she said to Simone Dietz that she would nail her in a coffin if Dietz tried to parachute into France, because she herself wanted to be the one to do that.

Dietz said that Weil had been in love with her friend Boris Souverine and there had been a rumor that she had had his child during the Spanish Civil War.

Weil had begun reading Eastern thought and in particular the Indian philosopher Milarepa in New York and said to her friend, "He is my mirror image."

She explained that there are mirror responses between two people speaking and usually hell is created in that mirror; but Milarepa produced just the opposite effect on Weil.

Convincingly, because reluctantly, Dietz told me that she had baptized Simone Weil in the hospital in Ashford, just hours before Weil died and just after a Catholic priest had refused to baptize her, declaring she was too proud.

Simone Dietz, already a Catholic convert, used the tap water from the sink in the sickroom.

I called the video *Simone Weil Avenue*—it was the first of five that I made—and showed it a few times in public—finally in New York near where it was first filmed.

+ + +

There was a conference at Columbia University called *Simone Weil: The Madness for Truth* held in the fall of 1999.

For those three days the sky was overcast, the air temperate and soggy, yellow leaves clattered underfoot, and rain was imminent. About one hundred people came to listen or participate. Long tables were set up in the front room in the brick Maison Française on the Columbia campus, and there was a gallery across the central hall with an installation of photocopied letters and pages from the notebooks of Simone Weil, photographs and other documents from her life, two videos running simultaneously, and a sound tunnel made of trash bags.

My video played in the outside hall. Someone damaged it before it began to play and after that it ran in defective lurches. I noticed no one watching it.

A body of work, going to work, on my way to work, I worked all day, they worked me, it was work!, what a piece of work, my first day of work, work is hell, why work?, it wasn't really work, all in a day's work, all work and no play, woman's work is never done, housework, working for shit, slave-work, piecework, factory work (industrial accident), coworker, works at home, homework, the division of labor produces an increase in the importance of each laborer, work for nothing, love and work, work stoppage, unrewarded work, every woman loves an idle man, work-hell, the workhouse, work ethic, workhorse, workaholic, does it work, I love my work, whatever works, a slave invented a handmill but the waterwheel was made by philosophers, the division of labor comes from the desire to barter and exchange, in dark times there is no work, work is dharma, poverty of spirit is facing reality without any myths, unworked land, the distance of a writer from the written is like the distance between labor and its given value, work for money, he likes my work, all exploitation has something in common with pornography, doubt and work, to have a woolen coat requires a sheep, work camp, what is my time worth, all the land has been worked and has a value, work beyond work.

On the first morning, the panel was almost entirely in French and devoted to the political thought and activity of Weil, who had been dubbed in her life "The Red Virgin." Here we heard about Weil's position on political parties during her sojourn in London. She was worrying over the future of political institutions in France because of her mistrust of any collective thought process.

She was disillusioned by institutions, including trade unions and parties, and blamed much of the problem on Nazism.

Weil said that working people "know everything; but outside work, they don't realize what knowledge they possess." This can only be remedied through the intervention of intellectuals, entering the labor field to educate the workers.

Simone Weil was still alive when I was born. At the time she was very attracted to Eastern philosophy. I can see why.

In Hindu terms she would be called *sannyasa*, someone who has heard the call to total renunciation and the acosmic life. She would have been seen as an enlightened wanderer, like a Beguine in France of the Middle Ages.

But in the contemporary West she was often judged as neurotic, anorexic, suicidal.

She wanted to live as a solitary, to the exclusion of the smallest luxury, to experience the effects of human helplessness, and to study affliction.

She mistrusted any ideology, dogma, or collective, believing that the mind is the true site of liberty.

Still, she felt that it was only through work that a person fully comes to terms with the human condition. Physical labor especially connects each person with the mechanisms of physical necessity.

If people are allowed to understand the tools they are using, they will work in a spirit of collaboration with nature. She saw no separation between contemplation and action, or wanted none.

This is the premise with which much of her later, more complex thought began.

For Weil, to be human is already to suffer. But the laboring body suffers all the more when the laborer has no access to the meaning of his task. What do the tools prove about natural law? Through education, and through work, a person should learn the relationship between the body and the tools she is using and the factory or corporation she works for. Working and learning will then be the same action and the alienation of the laborer from his daily work will lessen considerably.

What does a free person do except take the time to create a problem and solve it simultaneously?

Masses of disenfranchised factory workers and alienated, uprooted populations today might be interested in her positions on exploitation, labor, and education. In fact, some of them are—in Indonesia, Latin America, and elsewhere. What does a worker lack? Weil once asked this question and then answered: "The science of his affliction."

Sometimes she was nostalgic for the early trade unions that were devoted to the education of their members. She was a teacher of young girls for a while, and this job influenced her work on uprootedness.

She worked in a factory, where she saw firsthand that miserable education had created populations controlled by forces they couldn't react to, except instinctively.

To her it is ignorance that has made the grind of physical labor meaningless, a source of sorrow and indignity.

She gave a preferential role to teaching math to workers because it, more than anything, would help them understand that the mechanics of their tasks were actually working according to natural, internal (divine) laws.

Weil believed that the uncertainty principle was dangerous because it disordered the relationship between humans and the universe. She was appalled at the power that this theory conferred on the sciences. Why? Because she insisted that a person had to have a direct experience with the natural world or else be enslaved by it and hostile to it.

The conference—composed of intellectuals from France and the United States—ranged in wider and wider gyres around her life as a mid-century European and her ideas, about the Greeks, about Germany, about Marx and Christ and Judaism, becoming at certain points unpleasantly fixated on Weil's anti-Zionism and self-lacerating suicidal personality.

The session on Sunday morning dealt specifically with the Jewish question, and became quite contentious for a while.

However, Sylvère Lotringer gave a convincing talk on Weil's likeness to certain artists—Céline and Artaud—who foreshadowed in their work the cruelty about to be imported from Germany, and who heaped on themselves the loathing that would be projected out onto Jews across Europe.

He also described Weil as "one of the great minds of the 1930s and '40s, pushing her ideas to the limit without pity for anyone, in a kind of delirium."

In his analysis, to be chosen (a Jew) was to have no choice during those years. He helped to construct a bridge between those who were convinced of a virulent antisemitism in her thinking by suggesting there was irony, even play, in the bizarre way she denied being a Jew.

Weil was just as tough on the Roman Catholic Church as she was on Israel.

Yet her views on Judaism were dubbed by a Jewish scholar at Columbia an "unpardonable perfidy," as if she had been a German collaborator.

At its near closing-point the conference seemed to be divided between those who took a fundamentally Freudian and secular position on Weil (the masochistic, anorectic, antisemitic suicide) and those who took a more political and religious position (the radical freethinker—or anarchist—and mystical liberator).

+ + +

Wonderfully in keeping with Weil's commitment to issues of social justice, the last person to stand up to ask a question instead made a statement, in the workerlike person of an advocate for the homeless in Boston, who read a powerful statement of Weil's on the responsibility of each person for the other.

The conference then concluded with about twenty people walking down Riverside Drive to the building where Weil had lived for four months in 1943, and where a plaque in commemoration was celebrated with a melancholy poem by Eileen Myles, a passionate statement by a very old labor-union organizer who had fought in the Spanish Civil War, and the cutting of the ribbon by Weil's two nieces. It was the same building, of course, that I had filmed on that first day eight years before.

AFTER "PROLOGUE"

No one will ever know what experience—dreamed, imagined, read, lived—Simone Weil went through in order to write the prose poem called "Prologue." She admired Baudelaire. She loved fables and fairy tales. But does it matter to which category her piece belongs, falling as it did inside her journal?

Dimly it raises the question: How much of what she asserted came directly from experiences that she never mentions?

How much came from the daily bread of dream, imagination, reading, and life itself all combined?

For instance I once knew a man who was a poem.

He was, like the man in "Prologue," a person who disappeared suddenly.

He had no convictions, was a mass of contradictions, a pathological liar. If he said he was going to do something at a certain time, that was the one thing he was guaranteed not to do.

He lived in resistance to the culture's dream of a norm, refusing to obey any laws, keep any promises, say where he was to anyone, have an address, a phone or a bank card or an account. He was an addict, a petty criminal, an enthusiast. His memory was excellent, his intuitions about people and his information on them were uncanny.

He was handsome, well-dressed, ill physically and mentally, and uprooted and would have been homeless except for other people's kindness to him. He showed no gratitude for any of it.

Time for him swung from side to side and never went forward like a progress, but he collected pain-inspiring memories to nurse along with his addictions.

The only reading you could give of this man was a surface reading. There on his surface was his whole charisma. A close reading would end up in ever-evaporating signals like old subtitles or watermarks in papyrus. Nothing would add up. You would get a sequence of disconnected facts. Strangely this only made you more determined to make the narrative work—as a series of acts in which the missing parts were the coherent ones.

We hid away together in a stranger's flat for weeks. We drank wine at night and ate little, he roamed the streets and bars, collected money somewhere, called, didn't call, lied, disappeared, returned and broke all his promises, dismissing the fantasies of our future for the sake of his regular lonely beat.

He said to me three times, "I will ruin this," and these were the times he was happiest with me. I spent hours and hours dreading the days when he wouldn't call or remember me. There were so many of them and no way to find him without a phone or an address. His mind was like the traumatized star-soul whose discomposure Plato describes this way in the *Timaeus*:

> The circles were broken and disordered in every possible manner, so that when they moved they were tumbling to pieces and moved irrationally, at one time in a reverse direction, and then again obliquely, and then upside down as you might imagine a person who is upside down and has his head leaning upon the ground and his feet up against something in the air.

When the man who was a poem held me, he held me like the mother I had never had. He spoke aloud in the dark—long, embellished but credible stories poured forth from his childhood and late youth. This was his essence. The light bars from moving traffic outside slipped across the bare walls and in the next room Arab music played, and intermittently the Muslim call to prayer. Gray light at morning and soon after he would be on his way.

If I ever left him in the flat and went out, even for ten minutes, when I returned he would be gone. He took the opportunity to escape. He always lied, I guess, except once when he needed to be picked up from somewhere he was stranded, unable to walk because he was so sick.

Much of the time he was strong and good to look at and hold on to. I rarely saw him in daylight. He was afraid of the dark and listened to the news on the radio all night while I would sleep in the other room and only crawl into bed with him at the darkest hour before daybreak. I was ashamed of myself for loving someone so notoriously amoral, for truly soon he would be gone again, I never knew where.

Like a bigamist or a traitor, he had another life away from me that was better, if not as safe. Sometimes I wondered if he was gay, his disappearances were so complete and so rejecting.

Once in a while a report came in, from someone who didn't know about us, saying that he had been seen flirting with a woman in a bar; sleeping in a heap on the street; or quoting passages from newspapers as if they were his own opinions. I never heard anything good about him.

There is a pool between knowing and believing. Whatever I did know about this man who was a poem—something that could clear up my perplexity by giving me an actual fact—I didn't believe. I didn't choose not to believe. I just didn't.

What does belief mean in such a case? What does it ever mean?

You can know all the facts about a situation, you can even have an acknowledged intuition about how bad it all is, and still you believe that somehow the facts will pool their resources and reveal their ultimate worth.

You can know that someone doesn't love you and believe that they do.

You can know that someone will leave you and believe that they won't.

Belief is sister to delusion and insists on a positive outcome, no matter what. When someone justifies terrible behavior by someone else, it means that they love that person as they love themselves.

When someone doesn't justify the behavior but speaks ill of the person they are with, it means that they love that person more than the good.

If you are turned away by someone inscrutable whom you nonetheless love, what do you learn?

She wandered unfamiliar streets and couldn't find her way back, or forward. She was lost on earth. She loathed herself and blamed herself for his rejection of her—her sarcasm, her jealousy, doubt, impatience. Self-evaluation is what he taught her.

She had thought she was the good one, and he the reprobate and loser, but when he left it was the opposite. When she fell on her knees begging him to let her stay with him, it was really God she was imploring not to kill her belief.

The audible response was, Don't harden your heart.

Many people I loved died during that year, coincidentally. He didn't. So losing him was losing someone to life, a very different affair.

He was always out there wanting.

For a time I really tried to dissolve into black walls that lack perception. I feared seeing him as much as not seeing him. If someone resembled him far up the street, I literally trembled and veered.

But it was never the man who was a poem.

+ + +

His disappearance created a question in me. Maybe he did love me after all? Maybe the gestures that I remembered so intensely were indications of his love for me? Our tangled hours became like colorful reflections in a golden disk that I held up as an offering one day to the sun and one day to the candles.

All this was a prologue to belief.

Teacher can I have more time
To learn my lesson in?
No more daydreaming!
No more mistakes!
I promise I will pay attention
If I have one more day
To learn my lesson in

Did I walk that branch?
Did I hang from that lichen
Twig-green and hairy?
Did I swing? Did I rough up
My hands and laugh?
Was I scared when it was happening?
Was there an arm
To catch me—a protector better
Than any mother?

It was the sycamore nothing more

BIBLIOGRAPHY

Agamben, Giorgio. *Potentialities*. Stanford: Stanford University Press, 1999.

Arendt, Hannah. *Love and Saint Augustine*. Chicago: University of Chicago Press, 1996.

Beckett, Samuel. *The Complete Short Works*. New York: Grove Press, 1995.

Benjamin, Walter. *Illuminations*. New York: Harcourt Brace, 1968.

——. *Reflections*. New York: Harcourt Brace, 1978.

Boff, Clodovis. *Theology and Praxis*. New York: Orbis Books, 1987.

Cabaud, Jacques. *Simone Weil*. New York: Meredith Press, 1964.

Camus, Albert. *Notebooks (1942–1951)*. New York: Alfred Knopf, 1965.

de Certeau, Michel. *Heterologies*. Minneapolis: University of Minnesota, 1993.

——. *The Mystic Fable*. Chicago: University of Chicago Press, 1992.

Florensky, Pavel. *Iconostasis*. New York: St. Vladimir's Seminary Press, 1996.

Freccero, John. *The Poetics of Conversion*. Cambridge: Harvard University Press, 1986.

Frye, Northrop. *The Great Code*. New York: Harcourt Brace, 1982.

Gutierrez, Gustavo. *A Theology of Liberation*. New York: Orbis, 1973.

Hacking, Ian. *The Taming of Chance*. Cambridge: Cambridge University Press, 1995.

Jonas, Hans. *The Gnostic Religion*. Boston: Beacon Press, 1958.

Karmel, Ilona. *An Estate of Memory*. Boston: Houghton Mifflin, 1969.

———. *Stephania*. Boston: Houghton Mifflin, 1953.

Levinas, Emmanuel. *The Levinas Reader*, edited by Sean Hand. Oxford, U.K.: Blackwell, 1989.

———. *Outside the Subject*. Stanford: Stanford University Press, 1994.

Metz, Johann Baptist. *A Passion for God*. Boston: Paulist Press, 1998.

Pannikar, Raimondo. *The Silence of God*. New York: Orbis, 1990.

Pasquini, John J. *Atheism and Salvation*. Lanham, Md.: University Press of America, 2000.

Rahner, Karl. *Foundations of Christian Faith*. New York: Crossroad, 1989.

Robinson, James, editor. *The Nag Hammadi Library*. New York: Harper and Row, 1978.

St. John of the Cross. *The Collected Works of St. John of the Cross*. Washington, D.C.: ICS Publications, 1991.

St. Teresa of Avila. *The Collected Works of St. Teresa of Avila*. Washington, D.C.: ICS Publications, 1980.

Scholem, Gershon. *Major Trends in Jewish Mysticism*. New York: Schocken Books, 1941.

Sells, Michael A. *The Mystical Languages of Unsaying*. Chicago: University of Chicago, 1994.

Stein, Edith. *The Collected Works*. Washington, D.C.: ICS Publications, 1986.

———. *The Science of the Cross*. Chicago: Henry Regnery, 1960.

———. *Selected Writings*. Tr. by Susanne Batzdorff. Springfield, Ill.: Templegate, 1991.

Weil, Simone. *Gravity and Grace*. New York: Putnam, 1952.

———. *The Notebooks*. Edinburgh: T. & A. Constable, 1956.

———. *Reflections on Philosophy*. Cambridge: Cambridge University Press, 1978.

———. *Waiting for God*. New York: Putnam, 1951.

Wilde, Lady [Francesca Speranza]. *Legends of Ancient Ireland.* London: Chatto and Windus, 1902.

Wyschogrod, Edith. *Saints and Postmodernism.* Chicago: University of Chicago, 1990.

Yerushalmi, Yosef Hayim. *Zakhor.* Seattle: University of Washington, 1999.

ACKNOWLEDGMENTS

Many thanks to the editors of *Raddle Moon, Crayon, Murmur, Poetics Journal, Fiction International, O/Ars, Brick, Enough,* the *Chicago Review, Contemporary Authors, Code of Signals, Moving Borders,* and *Mirror, Mirror on the Wall,* who published these essays or portions of them. Special thanks to Mary Margaret Sloan, Andrew Levy, Rick London, Michael Redhill, Susan Clark, Susan Moon, and Dunstan Morrissey, O.S.B. for their thoughtful editorial suggestions.

And happy thanks to Weston Jesuit School of Theology, Penny Janeway, Glenstal Abbey, and Emma Rothschild for providing me with places to work.

DESIGNER JESSICA GRUNWALD
COMPOSITOR BOOKMATTERS
TEXT JANSON
DISPLAY INTERSTATE
PRINTER AND BINDER THOMSON-SHORE